MW00907073

GOD'S OWN WORD
ON OUR FEARS

Compiled by Pastor Scott Markle

Shepherding the Flock Ministries

7971 Washington St. ❖ Melvin, MI 48454
(810) 378-5323
www.sheperdingtheflock.com

Copyright © 2013 by Pastor Scott Markle

God's Own Word: On Our Fears
Compiled by Pastor Scott Markle

Printed in the United States of America

ISBN 9780615903453

All rights reserved solely by the author.

All Bible quotations are from the King James Version of the Bible.

Shepherding the Flock Ministries
7971 Washington St.
Melvin, MI 48454
(810) 378-5323
www.shepherdingtheflock.com

CONTENTS

INTRODUCTION

The "God's Own Word" booklet series is intended to reveal only God's own Word on a particular matter. Each booklet provides a compilation of Biblical passages on a particular subject and categorizes those passages under a set of headings related to that subject. In addition, portions of each passage are highlighted in bold italics in order to point out the parts of the passage that are the most relevant to the subject. In this manner, the reader is instructed *by God's own Word*. I pray that these booklets may spiritually edify, exhort, and encourage your heart.

For the Excellency of the Knowledge of Christ Jesus our Lord,
Abiding in Christ, and Christ in us,
Pastor Scott Markle

Fear Thou Not

Genesis 15:1 - After these things the word of the LORD came unto Abram in a vision, saying, *Fear not*, Abram: *I am thy shield, and thy exceeding great reward.*

Genesis 21:14-15, 16b-19 - And Abraham rose up early in the morning, and took bread, and a bottle of water, and gave it unto Hagar, putting it on her shoulder, and the child, and sent her away: and she departed, and wandered in the wilderness of Beersheba. And the water was spent in the bottle, and she cast the child under one of the shrubs . . . . And she sat over against him, and lift up her voice, and wept. *And God heard the voice of the lad*; and the angel of God called to Hagar out of heaven, and said unto her, What aileth thee, Hagar? *Fear not; for God hath heard the voice of the lad where he is.* Arise, lift up the lad, and hold him in thine hand; *for I will make him a great nation.* And God opened her eyes, and she saw a well of water; and she went, and filled the bottle with water, *and gave the lad drink.*

Genesis 26:19-25 - And Isaac's servants digged in the valley, and found there a well of springing water. And the herdmen of Gerar did strive with Isaac's herdmen, saying, The water is ours: and he called the name of the well Esek; because they strove with him. And they digged another well, and strove for that also: and he called the name of it Sitnah. And he removed from thence, and digged another well; and for that they strove not: and he called the name of it Rehoboth; and he said, ***For now the LORD hath made room for us, and we shall be fruitful in the land.*** And he went up from thence to Beersheba. And the LORD appeared unto him the same night, and said, ***I am the God of Abraham thy father: fear not, for I am with thee, and will bless thee, and multiply thy seed for my servant Abraham's sake. And he builded an altar there, and called upon the name of the LORD, and pitched his tent there***: and there Isaac's servants digged a well.

Genesis 43:19-23 - And they came near to the steward of Joseph's house, and they communed with him at the door of the house, and said, O sir, we came indeed down at the first time to buy food: and it came to pass, when we came to the inn, that we opened our sacks, and, behold, every man's money was in the mouth of his sack, our money in full weight: and we have brought it again in our hand. And other money have we brought down in our hands to buy food: we cannot tell who put our money in our sacks. And he said, ***Peace be to you, fear not: your God, and the God of your father, hath given you treasure in your sacks***: I had your money. And he brought Simeon out unto them.

Genesis 46:1-4 - And Israel took his journey with all that he had, and came to Beersheba, ***and offered sacrifices unto the God of his father Isaac.*** And God spake unto Israel in the visions of the night, and said, Jacob, Jacob. And he said, Here am I. ***And he said, I am God, the God of thy father: fear not to go down into Egypt; for I will there make of thee a great nation: I will go down with thee into Egypt; and I will also surely bring thee up again***: and Joseph shall put his hand upon thine eyes.

Genesis 50:15-21 - And when Joseph's brethren saw that their father was dead, they said, Joseph will peradventure hate us, and will certainly requite us all the evil which we did unto him. And they sent a messenger unto Joseph, saying, Thy father did command before he died, saying, So shall ye say unto Joseph, Forgive, I pray thee now, the trespass of thy brethren, and their sin; for they did unto thee evil: and now, we pray thee, forgive the trespass of the servants of the God of thy father. And Joseph wept when they spake unto him. And his brethren also went and fell down before his face; and they said, Behold, we be thy servants. And Joseph said unto them, *Fear not: for am I in the place of God? But as for you, ye thought evil against me; but God meant it unto good, to bring to pass, as it is this day, to save much people alive. Now therefore fear ye not: I will nourish you, and your little ones. And he comforted them, and spake kindly unto them.*

Exodus 14:10-14 - And when Pharaoh drew nigh, the children of Israel lifted up their eyes, and, behold, the Egyptians marched after them; *and they were sore afraid: and the children of Israel cried out unto the LORD.* And they said unto Moses, Because there were no graves in Egypt, hast thou taken us away to die in the wilderness? Wherefore hast thou dealt thus with us, to carry us forth out of Egypt? Is not this the word that we did tell thee in Egypt, saying, Let us alone, that we may serve the Egyptians? For it had been better for us to serve the Egyptians, than that we should die in the wilderness. And Moses said unto the people, *Fear ye not, stand still, and see the salvation of the LORD, which he will shew to you to day*: for the Egyptians whom ye have seen to day, ye shall see them again no more for ever. *The LORD shall fight for you, and ye shall hold your peace.*

Exodus 20:18-21 - And all the people saw the thunderings, and the lightnings, and the noise of the trumpet, and the mountain smoking: and when the people saw it, they removed, and stood afar off. And they said unto Moses, Speak thou with us, and we will hear: but let not God speak with us, lest we die. And Moses said unto the people, *Fear not: for God is come to prove you, and that his fear may be before your faces, that ye sin not.* And the people stood afar off, and Moses drew near unto the thick darkness where God was.

Numbers 14:6-10 - And Joshua the son of Nun, and Caleb the son of Jephunneh, which were of them that searched the land, rent their clothes: and they spake unto all the company of the children of Israel, saying, The land, which we passed through to search it, is an exceeding good land. *If the LORD delight in us, then he will bring us into this land, and give it us; a land which floweth with milk and honey. Only rebel not ye against the LORD, neither fear ye the people of the land; for they are bread for us: their defence is departed from them, and the LORD is with us: fear them not.* But all the congregation bade stone them with stones. And the glory of the LORD appeared in the tabernacle of the congregation before all the children of Israel.

Numbers 21:33-35 - And they turned and went up by the way of Bashan: and Og the king of Bashan went out against them, he, and all his people, to the battle at Edrei. And the LORD said unto Moses, *Fear him not: for I have delivered him into thy hand, and all his people, and his land*; and thou shalt do to him as thou didst unto Sihon king of the Amorites, which dwelt at Heshbon. *So they smote him, and his sons, and all his people, until there was none left him alive: and they possessed his land.*

Deuteronomy 1:16-17a - And I charged your judges at that time, saying, Hear the causes between your brethren, and judge righteously between every man and his brother, and the stranger that is with him. Ye shall not respect persons in judgment; but ye shall hear the small as well as the great; *ye shall not be afraid of the face of man; for the judgment is God's* . . . .

Deuteronomy 1:20-21, 26-31 - And I said unto you, Ye are come unto the mountain of the Amorites, which the LORD our God doth give unto us. *Behold, the LORD thy God hath set the land before thee: go up and possess it, as the LORD God of thy fathers hath said unto thee; fear not, neither be discouraged* . . . . Notwithstanding ye would not go up, but rebelled against the commandment of the LORD your God: and ye murmured in your tents, and said, Because the LORD hated us, he hath brought us forth out of the land of Egypt, to deliver us into the hand of the Amorites, to destroy us. Whither shall we go up? *Our brethren have discouraged our heart, saying, The people is greater and taller than we; the cities are great and walled up to heaven*; and moreover we have seen the sons of the Anakims there. *Then I said unto you, Dread not, neither be afraid of them. The LORD your God which goeth before you, he shall fight for you*, according to all that he did for you in Egypt before your eyes; and in the wilderness, *where thou hast seen how that the LORD thy God bare thee, as a man doth bear his son, in all the way that ye went, until ye came into this place.*

Deuteronomy 3:1-3 - Then we turned, and went up the way to Bashan: and Og the king of Bashan came out against us, he and all his people, to battle at Edrei. And the LORD said unto me, *Fear him not: for I will deliver him, and all his people, and his land, into thy hand*; and thou shalt do unto him as thou didst unto Sihon king of the Amorites, which dwelt at Heshbon. *So the LORD our God delivered into our hands Og also, the king of Bashan, and all his people: and we smote him until none was left to him remaining.*

Deuteronomy 3:21-22 - And I commanded Joshua at that time, saying, Thine eyes have seen all that the LORD your God hath done unto these two kings: so shall the LORD do unto all the kingdoms whither thou passest. *Ye shall not fear them: for the LORD your God he shall fight for you.*

Deuteronomy 7:17-21 - If thou shalt say in thine heart, These nations are more than I; how can I dispossess them? *Thou shalt not be afraid of them: but shalt well remember what the LORD thy God did unto Pharaoh, and unto all Egypt; the great temptations which thine eyes saw, and the signs, and the wonders, and the mighty hand, and the stretched out arm, whereby the LORD thy God brought thee out: so shall the LORD thy God do unto all the people of whom thou art afraid.* Moreover the LORD thy God will send the hornet among them, until they that are left, and hide themselves from thee, be destroyed. *Thou shalt not be affrighted at them: for the LORD thy God is among you, a mighty God and terrible.*

Deuteronomy 18:20-22 - But the prophet, which shall presume to speak a word in my name, which I have not commanded him to speak, or that shall speak in the name of other gods, even that prophet shall die. And if thou say in thine heart, How shall we know the word which the LORD hath not spoken? When a prophet speaketh in the name of the LORD, if the thing follow not, nor come to pass, *that is the thing which the LORD hath not spoken, but the prophet hath spoken it presumptuously: thou shalt not be afraid of him.*

Deuteronomy 20:1-4 - *When thou goest out to battle against thine enemies, and seest horses, and chariots, and a people more than thou, be not afraid of them: for the* LORD *thy God is with thee*, which brought thee up out of the land of Egypt. And it shall be, when ye are come nigh unto the battle, that the priest shall approach and speak unto the people, and shall say unto them, *Hear, O Israel, ye approach this day unto battle against your enemies: let not your hearts faint, fear not, and do not tremble, neither be ye terrified because of them; for the* LORD *your God is he that goeth with you, to fight for you against your enemies, to save you.*

Deuteronomy 31:3-8 - *The* LORD *thy God, he will go over before thee, and he will destroy these nations from before thee*, and thou shalt possess them: and Joshua, he shall go over before thee, as the LORD hath said. And the LORD shall do unto them as he did to Sihon and to Og, kings of the Amorites, and unto the land of them, whom he destroyed. *And the* LORD *shall give them up before your face*, that ye may do unto them according unto all the commandments which I have commanded you. *Be strong and of a good courage, fear not, nor be afraid of them: for the* LORD *thy God, he it is that doth go with thee; he will not fail thee, nor forsake thee.* And Moses called unto Joshua, and said unto him in the sight of all Israel, Be strong and of a good courage: for thou must go with this people unto the land which the LORD hath sworn unto their fathers to give them; and thou shalt cause them to inherit it. *And the* LORD, *he it is that doth go before thee; he will be with thee, he will not fail thee, neither forsake thee: fear not, neither be dismayed.*

Joshua 1:1-2, 5-9 - Now after the death of Moses the servant of the LORD it came to pass, that the LORD spake unto Joshua the son of Nun, Moses' minister, saying, Moses my servant is dead; now therefore arise, go over this Jordan, thou, and all this people, unto the land which I do give to them, even to the children of Israel . . . . *There shall not any man be able to stand before thee all the days of thy life: as I was with Moses, so I will be with thee: I will not fail thee, nor forsake thee. Be strong and of a good courage*: for unto this people shalt thou divide for an inheritance the land, which I sware unto their fathers to give them. *Only be thou strong and very courageous, that thou mayest observe to do according to all the law, which Moses my servant commanded thee: turn not from it to the right hand or to the left*, that thou mayest prosper whithersoever thou goest. *This book of the law shall not depart out of thy mouth; but thou shalt meditate therein day and night, that thou mayest observe to do according to all that is written therein*: for then thou shalt make thy way prosperous, and then thou shalt have good success. *Have not I commanded thee? Be strong and of a good courage; be not afraid, neither be thou dismayed: for the LORD thy God is with thee whithersoever thou goest.*

Joshua 8:1 - *And the LORD said unto Joshua, Fear not, neither be thou dismayed*: take all the people of war with thee, and arise, go up to Ai: *see, I have given into thy hand the king of Ai, and his people, and his city, and his land.*

Joshua 10:7-14, 25 - So Joshua ascended from Gilgal, he, and all the people of war with him, and all the mighty men of valour. *And the LORD said unto Joshua, Fear them not: for I have delivered them into thine hand; there shall not a man of them stand before thee.* Joshua therefore came unto them suddenly, and went up from Gilgal all night. *And the LORD discomfited them before Israel, and slew them with a great slaughter at Gibeon, and chased them along the way that goeth up to Bethhoron, and smote them to Azekah, and unto Makkedah.* And it came to pass, as they fled from before Israel, and were in the going down to Bethhoron, *that the LORD cast down great stones from heaven upon them unto Azekah, and they died: they were more which died with hailstones than they whom the children of Israel slew with the sword.* Then spake Joshua to the LORD in the day when the LORD delivered up the Amorites before the children of Israel, and he said in the sight of Israel, Sun, stand thou still upon Gibeon; and thou, Moon, in the valley of Ajalon. And the sun stood still, and the moon stayed, until the people had avenged themselves upon their enemies. Is not this written in the book of Jasher? So the sun stood still in the midst of heaven, and hasted not to go down about a whole day. And there was no day like that before it or after it, that the LORD hearkened unto the voice of a man: *for the LORD fought for Israel* . . . . *And Joshua said unto them, Fear not, nor be dismayed, be strong and of good courage: for thus shall the LORD do to all your enemies against whom ye fight.*

Joshua 11:4-6 - And they went out, they and all their hosts with them, much people, even as the sand that is upon the sea shore in multitude, with horses and chariots very many. And when all these kings were met together, they came and pitched together at the waters of Merom, to fight against Israel. *And the LORD said unto Joshua, Be not afraid because of them: for to morrow about this time will I deliver them up all slain before Israel*: thou shalt hough their horses, and burn their chariots with fire.

Judges 6:22-24 - And when Gideon perceived that he was an angel of the LORD, Gideon said, Alas, O Lord GOD! For because I have seen an angel of the LORD face to face. *And the LORD said unto him, Peace be unto thee; fear not: thou shalt not die. Then Gideon built an altar there unto the LORD, and called it Jehovahshalom* [The LORD send peace]: unto this day it is yet in Ophrah of the Abiezrites.

1 Samuel 12:16-21 - Now therefore stand and see this great thing, which the LORD will do before your eyes. Is it not wheat harvest to day? I will call unto the LORD, and he shall send thunder and rain; that ye may perceive and see that your wickedness is great, which ye have done in the sight of the LORD, in asking you a king. So Samuel called unto the LORD; and the LORD sent thunder and rain that day: *and all the people greatly feared the LORD and Samuel. And all the people said unto Samuel, Pray for thy servants unto the LORD thy God, that we die not: for we have added unto all our sins this evil, to ask us a king. And Samuel said unto the people, Fear not: ye have done all this wickedness: yet turn not aside from following the LORD, but serve the LORD with all your heart; and turn ye not aside: for then should ye go after vain things, which cannot profit nor deliver; for they are vain.*

1 Chronicles 22:11-13 - *Now, my son, the LORD be with thee*; and prosper thou, and build the house of the LORD thy God, as he hath said of thee. *Only the LORD give thee wisdom and understanding, and give thee charge concerning Israel, that thou mayest keep the law of the LORD thy God.* Then shalt thou prosper, if thou takest heed to fulfil the statutes and judgments which the LORD charged Moses with concerning Israel: *be strong, and of good courage; dread not, nor be dismayed.*

1 Chronicles 28:20 - And David said to Solomon his son, *Be strong and of good courage, and do it: fear not, nor be dismayed: for the LORD God, even my God, will be with thee; he will not fail thee, nor forsake thee, until thou hast finished all the work for the service of the house of the LORD.*

1 Kings 17:8-14 - And the word of the LORD came unto him, saying, Arise, get thee to Zarephath, which belongeth to Zidon, and dwell there: *behold, I have commanded a widow woman there to sustain thee.* So he arose and went to Zarephath. And when he came to the gate of the city, behold, the widow woman was there gathering of sticks: and he called to her, and said, Fetch me, I pray thee, a little water in a vessel, that I may drink. And as she was going to fetch it, he called to her, and said, Bring me, I pray thee, a morsel of bread in thine hand. *And she said, As the LORD thy God liveth, I have not a cake, but an handful of meal in a barrel, and a little oil in a cruse: and, behold, I am gathering two sticks, that I may go in and dress it for me and my son, that we may eat it, and die. And Elijah said unto her, Fear not; go and do as thou hast said: but make me thereof a little cake first, and bring it unto me, and after make for thee and for thy son. For thus saith the LORD God of Israel, The barrel of meal shall not waste, neither shall the cruse of oil fail, until the day that the LORD sendeth rain upon the earth.*

2 Chronicles 20:1, 3-4, 14-22 - It came to pass after this also, that the children of Moab, and the children of Ammon, and with them other beside the Ammonites, came against Jehoshaphat to battle . . . . *And Jehoshaphat feared, and set himself to seek the LORD, and proclaimed a fast throughout all Judah. And Judah gathered themselves together, to ask help of the LORD: even out of all* *the cities of Judah they came to seek the LORD . . . .* Then upon Jahaziel the son of Zechariah, the son of Benaiah, the son of Jeiel, the son of Mattaniah, a Levite of the sons of Asaph, came the Spirit of the LORD in the midst of the congregation; and he said, Hearken ye, all Judah, and ye inhabitants of Jerusalem, and thou king Jehoshaphat, *Thus saith the LORD unto you, Be not afraid nor dismayed by reason of this great multitude; for the battle is not yours, but God's.* To morrow go ye down against them: behold, they come up by the cliff of Ziz; and ye shall find them at the end of the brook, before the wilderness of Jeruel. *Ye shall not need to fight in this battle: set yourselves, stand ye still, and see the salvation of the LORD with you, O Judah and Jerusalem: fear not, nor be dismayed; to mor-row go out against them: for the LORD will be with you. And Jehoshaphat bowed his head with his face to the ground: and all Judah and the inhabitants of Jerusalem fell before the LORD, worshipping the LORD. And the Levites, of the children of the Kohathites, and of the chil-dren of the Korhites, stood up to praise the LORD God of Israel with a loud voice on high.* And they rose early in the morning, and went forth into the wilderness of Tekoa: and as they went forth, Jehoshaphat stood and said, Hear me, O Judah, and ye inhabitants of Jerusalem; *Believe in the LORD your God, so shall ye be established; believe his prophets, so shall ye prosper.* And when he had consulted with the people, *he appointed singers unto the LORD, and that should praise the beauty of holiness, as they went out before the army, and to say, Praise the LORD; for his mercy endureth for ever. And when they began to sing and to praise, the LORD set ambushments against the children of Ammon, Moab, and mount Seir*, which were come against Judah; and they were smitten.

2 Kings 6:8-17 - Then the king of Syria warred against Israel, and took counsel with his servants, saying, In such and such a place shall be my camp. And the man of God sent unto the king of Israel, saying, Beware that thou pass not such a place; for thither the Syrians are come down. And the king of Israel sent to the place which the man of God told him and warned him of, and saved himself there, not once nor twice. Therefore the heart of the king of Syria was sore troubled for this thing; and he called his servants, and said unto them, Will ye not shew me which of us is for the king of Israel? And one of his servants said, None, my lord, O king: but Elisha, the prophet that is in Israel, telleth the king of Israel the words that thou speakest in thy bed-chamber. And he said, Go and spy where he is, that I may send and fetch him. And it was told him, saying, Behold, he is in Dothan. Therefore sent he thither horses, and chariots, and a great host: and they came by night, and compassed the city about. *And when the servant of the man of God was risen early, and gone forth, behold, an host compassed the city both with horses and chariots. And his servant said unto him, Alas, my master! How shall we do? And he answered, Fear not: for they that be with us are more than they that be with them. And Elisha prayed, and said, LORD, I pray thee, open his eyes, that he may see. And the LORD opened the eyes of the young man; and he saw: and, behold, the mountain was full of horses and chariots of fire round about Elisha.*

Isaiah 7:1-9 - And it came to pass in the days of Ahaz the son of Jotham, the son of Uzziah, king of Judah, that Rezin the king of Syria, and Pekah the son of Remaliah, king of Israel, went up toward Jerusalem to war against it, but could not prevail against it. And it was told the house of David, saying, Syria is confederate with Ephraim. *And his heart was moved, and the heart of his people, as the trees* *of the wood are moved with the wind.* Then said the LORD unto Isaiah, Go forth now to meet Ahaz, thou, and Shearjashub thy son, at the end of the conduit of the upper pool in the highway of the fuller's field; and say unto him, *Take heed, and be quiet; fear not, neither be fainthearted for the two tails of these smoking firebrands, for the fierce anger of Rezin with Syria, and of the son of Remaliah.* Because Syria, Ephraim, and the son of Remaliah, have taken evil counsel against thee, saying, Let us go up against Judah, and vex it, and let us make a breach therein for us, and set a king in the midst of it, even the son of Tabeal: *thus saith the Lord GOD, It shall not stand, neither shall it come to pass.* For the head of Syria is Damascus, and the head of Damascus is Rezin; and within threescore and five years shall Ephraim be broken, that it be not a people. And the head of Ephraim is Samaria, and the head of Samaria is Remaliah's son. *If ye will not believe, surely ye shall not be established.*

Isaiah 10:24-27, 33 - Therefore thus saith the Lord GOD of hosts, *O my people that dwellest in Zion, be not afraid of the Assyrian*: he shall smite thee with a rod, and shall lift up his staff against thee, after the manner of Egypt. *For yet a very little while, and the indignation shall cease, and mine anger in their destruction. And the LORD of hosts shall stir up a scourge for him according to the slaughter of Midian at the rock of Oreb*: and as his rod was upon the sea, so shall he lift it up after the manner of Egypt. And it shall come to pass in that day, that his burden shall be taken away from off thy shoulder, and his yoke from off thy neck, and the yoke shall be destroyed because of the anointing . . . . *Behold, the Lord, the LORD of hosts, shall lop the bough with terror: and the high ones of stature shall be hewn down, and the haughty shall be humbled.*

2 Kings 18:9, 17a, 28-33, 35; 19:1-7, 35 - And it came to pass in the fourth year of king Hezekiah, which was the seventh year of Hoshea son of Elah king of Israel, that Shalmaneser king of Assyria came up against Samaria, and besieged it . . . . And the king of Assyria sent Tartan and Rabsaris and Rabshakeh from Lachish to king Hezekiah with a great host against Jerusalem . . . . Then Rabshakeh stood and cried with a loud voice in the Jews' language, and spake, saying, Hear the word of the great king, the king of Assyria: Thus saith the king, Let not Hezekiah deceive you: for he shall not be able to deliver you out of his hand: *neither let Hezekiah make you trust in the LORD, saying, The LORD will surely deliver us*, and this city shall not be delivered into the hand of the king of Assyria. Hearken not to Hezekiah: for thus saith the king of Assyria, Make an agreement with me by a present, and come out to me, and then eat ye every man of his own vine, and every one of his fig tree, and drink ye every one the waters of his cistern: until I come and take you away to a land like your own land, a land of corn and wine, a land of bread and vine-yards, a land of oil olive and of honey, that ye may live, and not die: *and hearken not unto Hezekiah, when he per-suadeth you, saying, The LORD will deliver us*. Hath any of the gods of the nations delivered at all his land out of the hand of the king of Assyria? . . . *Who are they among all the gods of the countries, that have delivered their country out of mine hand, that the LORD should deliver Jerusalem out of mine hand?* . . . And it came to pass, when king Hezekiah heard it, that he rent his clothes, and covered himself with sackcloth, and went into the house of the LORD. And he sent Eliakim, which was over the house-hold, and Shebna the scribe, and the elders of the priests, covered with sackcloth, to Isaiah the prophet the son of Amoz. And they said unto him, Thus saith Hezekiah, This day is a day of trouble, and of rebuke, and blasphemy: for the children are come to the birth, and there is not strength to bring forth. *It may be the LORD thy God will hear all the words of Rabshakeh, whom the king of Assyria his master hath sent to reproach the living God; and will reprove the words which the LORD thy God hath heard*: wherefore lift up thy prayer for the remnant that are left. So the servants of king Hezekiah came to Isaiah. And Isaiah said unto them, Thus shall ye say to your master, *Thus saith the LORD, Be not afraid of the words which thou hast heard, with which the servants of the king of Assyria have blasphemed me. Behold, I will send a blast upon him, and he shall hear a rumour, and shall return to his own land; and I will cause him to fall by the sword in his own land . . . . And it came to pass that night, that the angel of the LORD went out, and smote in the camp of the Assyrians an hundred fourscore and five thousand*: and when they arose early in the morning, behold, they were all dead corpses.

2 Chronicles 32:7-8 - *Be strong and courageous, be not afraid nor dismayed for the king of Assyria, nor for all the multitude that is with him: for there be more with us than with him: with him is an arm of flesh; but with us is the LORD our God to help us, and to fight our battles.* And the people rested themselves upon the words of Hezekiah king of Judah.

Jeremiah 42:7-12 - And it came to pass after ten days, that the word of the LORD came unto Jeremiah. Then called he Johanan the son of Kareah, and all the captains of the forces which were with him, and all the people from the least even to the greatest, and said unto them, Thus saith the LORD, the God of Israel, unto whom ye sent me to present your supplication before him; *If ye will still abide in this land, then will I build you, and not pull you down,* *and I will plant you, and not pluck you up: for I repent me of the evil that I have done unto you. Be not afraid of the king of Babylon, of whom ye are afraid; be not afraid of him, saith the LORD: for I am with you to save you, and to deliver you from his hand. And I will shew mercies unto you, that he may have mercy upon you, and cause you to return to your own land.*

Haggai 2:4-9 - *Yet now be strong*, O Zerubbabel, saith the LORD; *and be strong*, O Joshua, son of Josedech, the high priest; *and be strong, all ye people of the land, saith the LORD, and work: for I am with you, saith the LORD of hosts*: according to the word that I covenanted with you when ye came out of Egypt, *so my spirit remaineth among you: fear ye not.* For thus saith the LORD of hosts; Yet once, it is a little while, and I will shake the heavens, and the earth, and the sea, and the dry land; and I will shake all nations, and the desire of all nations shall come: *and I will fill this house with glory, saith the LORD of hosts.* The silver is mine, and the gold is mine, saith the LORD of hosts. *The glory of this latter house shall be greater than of the former, saith the LORD of hosts: and in this place will I give peace, saith the LORD of hosts.*

Nehemiah 4:7-15 - But it came to pass, that when Sanballat, and Tobiah, and the Arabians, and the Ammonites, and the Ashdodites, heard that the walls of Jerusalem were made up, and that the breaches began to be stopped, then they were very wroth, and conspired all of them together to come and to fight against Jerusalem, and to hinder it. *Nevertheless we made our prayer unto our God, and set a watch against them day and night, because of them.* And Judah said, The strength of the bearers of burdens is decayed, and there is much rubbish; so that we are not able to build the wall. And our adversaries said, They shall not know, neither see, till we come in the midst among them, and slay them, and cause the work to cease. And it came to pass, that when the Jews which dwelt by them came, they said unto us ten times, From all places whence ye shall return unto us they will be upon you. Therefore set I in the lower places behind the wall, and on the higher places, I even set the people after their families with their swords, their spears, and their bows. And I looked, and rose up, and said unto the nobles, and to the rulers, and to the rest of the people, *Be not ye afraid of them: remember the Lord, which is great and terrible, and fight for your brethren, your sons, and your daughters, your wives, and your houses.* And it came to pass, when our enemies heard that it was known unto us, *and God had brought their counsel to nought*, that we returned all of us to the wall, every one unto his work.

Psalm 49:16-20 - *Be not thou afraid when one is made rich, when the glory of his house is increased*; for when he dieth he shall carry nothing away: his glory shall not descend after him. Though while he lived he blessed his soul: and men will praise thee, when thou doest well to thyself. He shall go to the generation of his fathers; they shall never see light. Man that is in honour, and understandeth not, is like the beasts that perish.

Proverbs 3:25-26 - *Be not afraid of sudden fear, neither of the desolation of the wicked, when it cometh. For the LORD shall be thy confidence, and shall keep thy foot from being taken.*

Isaiah 8:11-15 - For the LORD spake thus to me with a strong hand, and instructed me that I should not walk in the way of this people, saying, *Say ye not, A confederacy, to all them to whom this people shall say, A confederacy; neither fear ye their fear, nor be afraid. Sanctify the*

LORD *of hosts himself; and let him be your fear, and let him be your dread.* *And he shall be for a sanctuary*; but for a stone of stumbling and for a rock of offence to both the houses of Israel, for a gin and for a snare to the inhabitants of Jerusalem. And many among them shall stumble, and fall, and be broken, and be snared, and be taken.

Isaiah 35:3-10 - *Strengthen ye the weak hands, and confirm the feeble knees. Say to them that are of a fearful heart, Be strong, fear not: behold, your God will come with vengeance, even God with a recompence; he will come and save you.* Then the eyes of the blind shall be opened, and the ears of the deaf shall be unstopped. Then shall the lame man leap as an hart, and the tongue of the dumb sing: for in the wilderness shall waters break out, and streams in the desert. And the parched ground shall become a pool, and the thirsty land springs of water: in the habitation of dragons, where each lay, shall be grass with reeds and rushes. And an highway shall be there, and a way, and it shall be called The way of holiness; the unclean shall not pass over it; but it shall be for those: the wayfaring men, though fools, shall not err therein. No lion shall be there, nor any ravenous beast shall go up thereon, it shall not be found there; but the redeemed shall walk there: and the ransomed of the LORD shall return, and come to Zion with songs and everlasting joy upon their heads: they shall obtain joy and gladness, and sorrow and sighing shall flee away.

Isaiah 40:9 - *O Zion, that bringest good tidings, get thee up into the high mountain; O Jerusalem, that bringest good tidings, lift up thy voice with strength; lift it up, be not afraid; say unto the cities of Judah, Behold your God!*

Isaiah 41:8-14 - *But thou, Israel, art my servant, Jacob whom I have chosen, the seed of Abraham my friend.* Thou whom I have taken from the ends of the earth, and called thee from the chief men thereof, and said unto thee, *Thou art my servant; I have chosen thee, and not cast thee away. Fear thou not; for I am with thee: be not dismayed; for I am thy God: I will strengthen thee; yea, I will help thee; yea, I will uphold thee with the right hand of my righteousness.* Behold, all they that were incensed against thee shall be ashamed and confounded: they shall be as nothing; and they that strive with thee shall perish. Thou shalt seek them, and shalt not find them, even them that contended with thee: they that war against thee shall be as nothing, and as a thing of nought. *For I the LORD thy God will hold thy right hand, saying unto thee, Fear not; I will help thee. Fear not, thou worm Jacob, and ye men of Israel; I will help thee, saith the LORD, and thy redeemer, the Holy One of Israel.*

Isaiah 43:1-7 - *But now thus saith the LORD that created thee, O Jacob, and he that formed thee, O Israel, Fear not: for I have redeemed thee, I have called thee by thy name; thou art mine. When thou passest through the waters, I will be with thee; and through the rivers, they shall not overflow thee: when thou walkest through the fire, thou shalt not be burned; neither shall the flame kindle upon thee. For I am the LORD thy God, the Holy One of Israel, thy Saviour*: I gave Egypt for thy ransom, Ethiopia and Seba for thee. *Since thou wast precious in my sight, thou hast been honourable, and I have loved thee*: therefore will I give men for thee, and people for thy life. *Fear not: for I am with thee*: I will bring thy seed from the east, and gather thee from the west; I will say to the north, Give up; and to the south, Keep not back: bring my sons from far, and my daughters from the ends of the earth; even every one that is called by my name: for I have created him for my glory, I have formed him; yea, I have made him.

Isaiah 44:1-4, 6-8 - *Yet now hear, O Jacob my servant; and Israel, whom I have chosen: Thus saith the* LORD *that made thee, and formed thee from the womb, which will help thee; Fear not, O Jacob, my servant; and thou, Jesurun, whom I have chosen. For I will pour water upon him that is thirsty, and floods upon the dry ground: I will pour my spirit upon thy seed, and my blessing upon thine offspring: and they shall spring up as among the grass, as willows by the water courses . . . . Thus saith the* LORD *the King of Israel, and his redeemer the* LORD *of hosts; I am the first, and I am the last; and beside me there is no God. And who, as I, shall call, and shall declare it, and set it in order for me, since I appointed the ancient people?* And the things that are coming, and shall come, let them shew unto them. *Fear ye not, neither be afraid: have not I told thee from that time, and have declared it?* Ye are even my witnesses. Is there a God beside me? *Yea, there is no God; I know not any.*

Isaiah 51:7-8 - *Hearken unto me, ye that know righteousness, the people in whose heart is my law; fear ye not the reproach of men, neither be ye afraid of their revilings.* For the moth shall eat them up like a garment, and the worm shall eat them like wool: *but my righteousness shall be for ever, and my salvation from generation to generation.*

Isaiah 54:1-5 - Sing, O barren, thou that didst not bear; break forth into singing, and cry aloud, thou that didst not travail with child: for more are the children of the desolate than the children of the married wife, saith the LORD. Enlarge the place of thy tent, and let them stretch forth the curtains of thine habitations: spare not, lengthen thy cords, and strengthen thy stakes; for thou shalt break forth on the right hand and on the left; and thy seed shall inherit the Gentiles, and make the desolate cities to be inhabited. *Fear not; for thou shalt not be ashamed: neither be thou confounded; for thou shalt not be put to shame: for thou shalt forget the shame of thy youth, and shalt not remember the reproach of thy widowhood any more. For thy Maker is thine husband; the LORD of hosts is his name; and thy Redeemer the Holy One of Israel; The God of the whole earth shall he be called.*

Jeremiah 1:4-10, 17-19 - Then the word of the LORD came unto me, saying, Before I formed thee in the belly I knew thee; and before thou camest forth out of the womb I sanctified thee, and I ordained thee a prophet unto the nations. Then said I, Ah, Lord GOD! Behold, I cannot speak: for I am a child. But the LORD said unto me, Say not, I am a child: *for thou shalt go to all that I shall send thee, and whatsoever I command thee thou shalt speak. Be not afraid of their faces: for I am with thee to deliver thee, saith the LORD.* Then the LORD put forth his hand, and touched my mouth. And the LORD said unto me, Behold, I have put my words in thy mouth. See, I have this day set thee over the nations and over the kingdoms, to root out, and to pull down, and to destroy, and to throw down, to build, and to plant . . . . *Thou therefore gird up thy loins, and arise, and speak unto them all that I command thee: be not dismayed at their faces*, lest I confound thee before them. *For, behold, I have made thee this day a defenced city, and an iron pillar, and brasen walls against the whole land*, against the kings of Judah, against the princes thereof, against the priests thereof, and against the people of the land. *And they shall fight against thee; but they shall not prevail against thee; for I am with thee, saith the LORD, to deliver thee.*

Jeremiah 10:2-5 - *Thus saith the LORD, Learn not the way of the heathen, and be not dismayed at the signs of heaven; for the heathen are dismayed at them.* For the customs of the people are vain: for one cutteth a tree out of the forest, the work of the hands of the workman, with the axe. They deck it with silver and with gold; they fasten it with nails and with hammers, that it move not. They are upright as the palm tree, but speak not: they must needs be borne, because they cannot go. *Be not afraid of them; for they cannot do evil, neither also is it in them to do good.*

Jeremiah 30:10-11 - *Therefore fear thou not, O my servant Jacob, saith the LORD; neither be dismayed, O Israel: for, lo, I will save thee from afar, and thy seed from the land of their captivity; and Jacob shall return, and shall be in rest, and be quiet, and none shall make him afraid. For I am with thee, saith the LORD, to save thee*: though I make a full end of all nations whither I have scattered thee, *yet will I not make a full end of thee*: but I will correct thee in measure, and will not leave thee altogether unpunished.

Jeremiah 46:27-28 - *But fear not thou, O my servant Jacob, and be not dismayed, O Israel: for, behold, I will save thee from afar off, and thy seed from the land of their captivity; and Jacob shall return, and be in rest and at ease, and none shall make him afraid. Fear thou not, O Jacob my servant, saith the LORD: for I am with thee*; for I will make a full end of all the nations whither I have driven thee: *but I will not make a full end of thee*, but correct thee in measure; yet will I not leave thee wholly unpunished.

Lamentations 3:55-62 - I called upon thy name, O LORD, out of the low dungeon. Thou hast heard my voice: hide not thine ear at my breathing, at my cry. *Thou drewest*

near in the day that I called upon thee: thou saidst, Fear not. O Lord, thou hast pleaded the causes of my soul; thou hast redeemed my life. O LORD, thou hast seen my wrong: judge thou my cause. Thou hast seen all their vengeance and all their imaginations against me. Thou hast heard their reproach, O LORD, and all their imaginations against me; the lips of those that rose up against me, and their device against me all the day.

Ezekiel 2:3-8 - *And he said unto me, Son of man, I send thee to the children of Israel, to a rebellious nation that hath rebelled against me*: they and their fathers have transgressed against me, even unto this very day. For they are impudent children and stiffhearted. *I do send thee unto them; and thou shalt say unto them, Thus saith the Lord GOD.* And they, whether they will hear, or whether they will forbear, (for they are a rebellious house,) yet shall know that there hath been a prophet among them. *And thou, son of man, be not afraid of them, neither be afraid of their words, though briers and thorns be with thee, and thou dost dwell among scorpions: be not afraid of their words, nor be dismayed at their looks, though they be a rebellious house. And thou shalt speak my words unto them, whether they will hear, or whether they will forbear: for they are most rebellious.* But thou, son of man, hear what I say unto thee; *Be not thou rebellious like that rebellious house*: open thy mouth, and eat that I give thee.

Ezekiel 3:4-5, 7-9 - *And he said unto me, Son of man, go, get thee unto the house of Israel, and speak with my words unto them.* For thou art not sent to a people of a strange speech and of an hard language, but to the house of Israel . . . . But the house of Israel will not hearken unto thee; for they will not hearken unto me: for all the house of Israel are impudent and hardhearted. *Behold, I have made* *thy face strong against their faces, and thy forehead strong against their foreheads. As an adamant harder than flint have I made thy forehead: fear them not, neither be dismayed at their looks, though they be a rebellious house.*

Daniel 10:10-12, 15-19 - And, behold, an hand touched me, which set me upon my knees and upon the palms of my hands. And he said unto me, *O Daniel, a man greatly beloved*, understand the words that I speak unto thee, and stand upright: for unto thee am I now sent. *And when he had spoken this word unto me, I stood trembling. Then said he unto me, Fear not, Daniel: for from the first day that thou didst set thine heart to understand, and to chasten thyself before thy God, thy words were heard, and I am come for thy words* . . . . And when he had spoken such words unto me, I set my face toward the ground, and I became dumb. And, behold, one like the similitude of the sons of men touched my lips: then I opened my mouth, and spake, and said unto him that stood before me, O my lord, by the vision my sorrows are turned upon me, and I have retained no strength. For how can the servant of this my lord talk with this my lord? For as for me, straightway there remained no strength in me, neither is there breath left in me. Then there came again and touched me one like the appearance of a man, and he strengthened me, and said, *O man greatly beloved, fear not: peace be unto thee, be strong, yea, be strong.* And when he had spoken unto me, *I was strengthened*, and said, Let my lord speak; *for thou hast strengthened me*.

Joel 2:18-27 - Then will the LORD be jealous for his land, *and pity his people. Yea, the LORD will answer and say unto his people, Behold, I will send you corn, and wine, and oil, and ye shall be satisfied therewith: and I will no* *more make you a reproach among the heathen: but I will remove far off from you the northern army*, and will drive him into a land barren and desolate, with his face toward the east sea, and his hinder part toward the utmost sea, and his stink shall come up, and his ill savour shall come up, because he hath done great things. *Fear not, O land; be glad and rejoice: for the LORD will do great things. Be not afraid, ye beasts of the field: for the pastures of the wilderness do spring, for the tree beareth her fruit, the fig tree and the vine do yield their strength. Be glad then, ye children of Zion, and rejoice in the LORD your God*: for he hath given you the former rain moderately, and he will cause to come down for you the rain, the former rain, and the latter rain in the first month. And the floors shall be full of wheat, and the fats shall overflow with wine and oil. *And I will restore to you the years* that the locust hath eaten, the cankerworm, and the caterpiller, and the palmerworm, my great army which I sent among you. *And ye shall eat in plenty, and be satisfied, and praise the name of the LORD your God, that hath dealt wondrously with you: and my people shall never be ashamed. And ye shall know that I am in the midst of Israel, and that I am the LORD your God, and none else: and my people shall never be ashamed.*

Zephaniah 3:14-17 - *Sing, O daughter of Zion; shout, O Israel; be glad and rejoice with all the heart, O daughter of Jerusalem. The LORD hath taken away thy judgments, he hath cast out thine enemy: the king of Israel, even the LORD, is in the midst of thee: thou shalt not see evil any more. In that day it shall be said to Jerusalem, Fear thou not: and to Zion, Let not thine hands be slack. The LORD thy God in the midst of thee is mighty; he will save, he will rejoice over thee with joy; he will rest in his love, he will joy over thee with singing.*

Zechariah 8:13-15 - And it shall come to pass, that as ye were a curse among the heathen, O house of Judah, and house of Israel; *so will I save you, and ye shall be a blessing: fear not, but let your hands be strong.* For thus saith the LORD of hosts; As I thought to punish you, when your fathers provoked me to wrath, saith the LORD of hosts, and I repented not: *so again have I thought in these days to do well unto Jerusalem and to the house of Judah: fear ye not.*

Luke 1:5-9, 11-17 - There was in the days of Herod, the king of Judaea, a certain priest named Zacharias, of the course of Abia: and his wife was of the daughters of Aaron, and her name was Elisabeth. And they were both righteous before God, walking in all the commandments and ordinances of the Lord blameless. And they had no child, because that Elisabeth was barren, and they both were now well stricken in years. And it came to pass, that while he executed the priest's office before God in the order of his course, according to the custom of the priest's office, his lot was to burn incense when he went into the temple of the Lord . . . . And there appeared unto him an angel of the Lord standing on the right side of the altar of incense. *And when Zacharias saw him, he was troubled, and fear fell upon him. But the angel said unto him, Fear not, Zacharias: for thy prayer is heard; and thy wife Elisabeth shall bear thee a son, and thou shalt call his name John. And thou shalt have joy and gladness; and many shall rejoice at his birth.* For he shall be great in the sight of the Lord, and shall drink neither wine nor strong drink; and he shall be filled with the Holy Ghost, even from his mother's womb. And many of the children of Israel shall he turn to the Lord their God. And he shall go before him in the spirit and power of Elias, to turn the hearts of the fathers to the children, and the disobedient to the wisdom of the just; to make ready a people prepared for the Lord.

Luke 1:26-33 - And in the sixth month the angel Gabriel was sent from God unto a city of Galilee, named Nazareth, to a virgin espoused to a man whose name was Joseph, of the house of David; and the virgin's name was Mary. And the angel came in unto her, and said, Hail, thou that art highly favoured, the Lord is with thee: blessed art thou among women. *And when she saw him, she was troubled at his saying*, and cast in her mind what manner of salutetion this should be. *And the angel said unto her, Fear not, Mary: for thou hast found favour with God. And, behold, thou shalt conceive in thy womb, and bring forth a son, and shalt call his name JESUS.* He shall be great, and shall be called the Son of the Highest: and the Lord God shall give unto him the throne of his father David: and he shall reign over the house of Jacob for ever; and of his kingdom there shall be no end.

Matthew 1:18-23 - Now the birth of Jesus Christ was on this wise: When as his mother Mary was espoused to Joseph, before they came together, she was found with child of the Holy Ghost. Then Joseph her husband, being a just man, and not willing to make her a publick example, was minded to put her away privily. But while he thought on these things, behold, the angel of the Lord appeared unto him in a dream, saying, *Joseph, thou son of David, fear not to take unto thee Mary thy wife: for that which is conceived in her is of the Holy Ghost. And she shall bring forth a son, and thou shalt call his name JESUS: for he shall save his people from their sins.* Now all this was done, that it might be fulfilled which was spoken of the Lord by the prophet, saying, *Behold, a virgin shall be with child, and shall bring forth a son, and they shall call his name Emmanuel, which being interpreted is, God with us.*

Luke 2:8-14 - And there were in the same country shepherds abiding in the field, keeping watch over their flock by night. And, lo, the angel of the Lord came upon them, and the glory of the Lord shone round about them: *and they were sore afraid. And the angel said unto them, Fear not: for, behold, I bring you good tidings of great joy, which shall be to all people. For unto you is born this day in the city of David a Saviour, which is Christ the Lord.* And this shall be a sign unto you; Ye shall find the babe wrapped in swaddling clothes, lying in a manger. *And suddenly there was with the angel a multitude of the heavenly host praising God, and saying, Glory to God in the highest, and on earth peace, good will toward men.*

Luke 5:3-11 - And he entered into one of the ships, which was Simon's, and prayed him that he would thrust out a little from the land. And he sat down, and taught the people out of the ship. Now when he had left speaking, he said unto Simon, Launch out into the deep, and let down your nets for a draught. And Simon answering said unto him, Master, we have toiled all the night, and have taken nothing: nevertheless at thy word I will let down the net. And when they had this done, they inclosed a great multitude of fishes: and their net brake. And they beckoned unto their partners, which were in the other ship, that they should come and help them. And they came, and filled both the ships, so that they began to sink. *When Simon Peter saw it, he fell down at Jesus' knees, saying, Depart from me; for I am a sinful man, O Lord.* For he was astonished, and all that were with him, at the draught of the fishes which they had taken: and so was also James, and John, the sons of Zebedee, which were partners with Simon. *And Jesus said unto Simon, Fear not; from henceforth thou shalt catch men.* And when they had brought their ships to land, *they forsook all, and followed him.*

Luke 8:41-42a, 49-50 - And, behold, there came a man named Jairus, and he was a ruler of the synagogue: and he fell down at Jesus' feet, and besought him that he would come into his house: for he had one only daughter, about twelve years of age, and she lay a dying . . . . While he yet spake, there cometh one from the ruler of the synagogue's house, saying to him, Thy daughter is dead; trouble not the Master. But when Jesus heard it, he answered him, saying, *Fear not: believe only*, and she shall be made whole. (See also Matthew 9:18-19, 23-26; Mark 5:22-24, 35-43)

Matthew 10:22-33 - *And ye shall be hated of all men for my name's sake*: but he that endureth to the end shall be saved. *But when they persecute you in this city, flee ye into another*: for verily I say unto you, Ye shall not have gone over the cities of Israel, till the Son of man be come. The disciple is not above his master, nor the servant above his lord. It is enough for the disciple that he be as his master, and the servant as his lord. If they have called the master of the house Beelzebub, how much more shall they call them of his household? *Fear them not therefore*: for there is nothing covered, that shall not be revealed; and hid, that shall not be known. *What I tell you in darkness, that speak ye in light: and what ye hear in the ear, that preach ye upon the housetops. And fear not them which kill the body, but are not able to kill the soul*: but rather fear him which is able to destroy both soul and body in hell. Are not two sparrows sold for a farthing? And one of them shall not fall on the ground without your Father. But the very hairs of your head are all numbered. *Fear ye not therefore, ye are of more value than many sparrows. Whosoever therefore shall confess me before men, him will I confess also before my Father which is in heaven.* But whosoever shall deny me before men, him will I also deny before my Father which is in heaven. (See also Luke 12:4-9)

Luke 12:22-34 - And he said unto his disciples, *Therefore I say unto you, Take no thought for your life, what ye shall eat; neither for the body, what ye shall put on.* The life is more than meat, and the body is more than raiment. Consider the ravens: for they neither sow nor reap; which neither have storehouse nor barn; and God feedeth them: how much more are ye better than the fowls? And which of you with taking thought can add to his stature one cubit? If ye then be not able to do that thing which is least, why take ye thought for the rest? Consider the lilies how they grow: they toil not, they spin not; and yet I say unto you, that Solomon in all his glory was not arrayed like one of these. *If then God so clothe the grass, which is to day in the field, and to morrow is cast into the oven; how much more will he clothe you, O ye of little faith? And seek not ye what ye shall eat, or what ye shall drink, neither be ye of doubtful mind.* For all these things do the nations of the world seek after: *and your Father knoweth that ye have need of these things. But rather seek ye the kingdom of God; and all these things shall be added unto you. Fear not, little flock; for it is your Father's good pleasure to give you the kingdom.* Sell that ye have, and give alms; provide yourselves bags which wax not old, a treasure in the heavens that faileth not, where no thief approacheth, neither moth corrupteth. For where your treasure is, there will your heart be also.

Matthew 14:22-32 - And straightway Jesus constrained his disciples to get into a ship, and to go before him unto the other side, while he sent the multitudes away. And when he had sent the multitudes away, he went up into a mountain apart to pray: and when the evening was come, he was there alone. But the ship was now in the midst of the sea, tossed with waves: for the wind was contrary. And in the fourth watch of the night Jesus went unto them, walking on the sea. *And when the disciples saw him walking on the sea, they were troubled, saying, It is a spirit; and they cried out for fear. But straightway Jesus spake unto them, saying, Be of good cheer; it is I; be not afraid.* And Peter answered him and said, Lord, if it be thou, bid me come unto thee on the water. And he said, Come. And when Peter was come down out of the ship, he walked on the water, to go to Jesus. *But when he saw the wind boisterous, he was afraid; and beginning to sink, he cried, saying, Lord, save me.* And immediately Jesus stretched forth his hand, and caught him, and said unto him, *O thou of little faith, wherefore didst thou doubt?* And when they were come into the ship, the wind ceased. (See also Mark 6:45-52; John 6:16-21)

Matthew 17:1-8 - And after six days Jesus taketh Peter, James, and John his brother, and bringeth them up into an high mountain apart, and was transfigured before them: and his face did shine as the sun, and his raiment was white as the light. And, behold, there appeared unto them Moses and Elias talking with him. Then answered Peter, and said unto Jesus, Lord, it is good for us to be here: if thou wilt, let us make here three tabernacles; one for thee, and one for Moses, and one for Elias. While he yet spake, behold, a bright cloud overshadowed them: and behold a voice out of the cloud, which said, This is my beloved Son, in whom I am well pleased; hear ye him. *And when the disciples heard it, they fell on their face, and were sore afraid. And Jesus came and touched them, and said, Arise, and be not afraid.* And when they had lifted up their eyes, they saw no man, save Jesus only. (See also Mark 9:2-10; Luke 9:28-36)

John 12:12-15 - On the next day much people that were come to the feast, when they heard that Jesus was coming to Jerusalem, took branches of palm trees, and went forth to meet him, and cried, Hosanna: Blessed is the King of Israel that cometh in the name of the Lord. And Jesus, when he had found a young ass, sat thereon; *as it is written, Fear not, daughter of Sion: behold, thy King cometh, sitting on an ass's colt.*

John 14:26-27 - But the Comforter, which is the Holy Ghost, whom the Father will send in my name, he shall teach you all things, and bring all things to your remembrance, whatsoever I have said unto you. *Peace I leave with you, my peace I give unto you: not as the world giveth, give I unto you. Let not your heart be troubled, neither let it be afraid.*

Matthew 28:1-10 - In the end of the sabbath, as it began to dawn toward the first day of the week, came Mary Magdalene and the other Mary to see the sepulchre. And, behold, there was a great earthquake: for the angel of the Lord descended from heaven, and came and rolled back the stone from the door, and sat upon it. His countenance was like lightning, and his raiment white as snow: *and for fear of him the keepers did shake, and became as dead men. And the angel answered and said unto the women, Fear not ye: for I know that ye seek Jesus, which was crucified. He is not here: for he is risen, as he said.* Come, see the place where the Lord lay. And go quickly, and tell his disciples that he is risen from the dead; and, behold, he goeth before you into Galilee; *there shall ye see him*: lo, I have told you. *And they departed quickly from the sepulchre with fear and great joy*; and did run to bring his disciples word. And as they went to tell his disciples, *behold, Jesus met them, saying, All hail*. And they came and held him by the feet, and worshipped him. *Then said Jesus unto them, Be not afraid: go tell my brethren that they go into Galilee, and there shall they see me.* (See also Mark 16:1-8; Luke 24:1-11)

Acts 18:9-10 - Then spake the Lord to Paul in the night by a vision, *Be not afraid, but speak, and hold not thy peace: for I am with thee, and no man shall set on thee to hurt thee*: for I have much people in this city.

Acts 27:14, 20-25 - But not long after there arose against it a tempestuous wind, called Euroclydon . . . . And when neither sun nor stars in many days appeared, and no small tempest lay on us, *all hope that we should be saved was then taken away.* But after long abstinence Paul stood forth in the midst of them, and said, Sirs, ye should have hearkened unto me, and not have loosed from Crete, and to have gained this harm and loss. *And now I exhort you to be of good cheer: for there shall be no loss of any man's life among you*, but of the ship. For there stood by me this night the angel of God, whose I am, and whom I serve, saying, *Fear not, Paul*; thou must be brought before Caesar: *and, lo, God hath given thee all them that sail with thee. Wherefore, sirs, be of good cheer: for I believe God, that it shall be even as it was told me.*

1 Peter 3:14-17 - *But and if ye suffer for righteousness' sake, happy are ye: and be not afraid of their terror, neither be troubled; but sanctify the Lord God in your hearts: and be ready always to give an answer to every man that asketh you a reason of the hope that is in you with meekness and fear: having a good conscience; that, whereas they speak evil of you, as of evildoers, they may be ashamed that falsely accuse your good conversation in Christ.* For it is better, if the will of God be so, that ye suffer for well doing, than for evil doing.

Revelation 1:12-18 - And I turned to see the voice that spake with me. And being turned, I saw seven golden candlesticks; and in the midst of the seven candlesticks one like unto the Son of man, clothed with a garment down to the foot, and girt about the paps with a golden girdle. His head and his hairs were white like wool, as white as snow; and his eyes were as a flame of fire; and his feet like unto fine brass, as if they burned in a furnace; and his voice as the sound of many waters. And he had in his right hand seven stars: and out of his mouth went a sharp twoedged sword: and his countenance was as the sun shineth in his strength. *And when I saw him, I fell at his feet as dead. And he laid his right hand upon me, saying unto me, Fear not; I am the first and the last: I am he that liveth, and was dead; and, behold, I am alive for evermore, Amen; and have the keys of hell and of death.*

Revelation 2:8-10 - And unto the angel of the church in Smyrna write; These things saith the first and the last, which was dead, and is alive; *I know thy works, and tribulation, and poverty*, (but thou art rich) and I know the blasphemy of them which say they are Jews, and are not, but are the synagogue of Satan. *Fear none of those things which thou shalt suffer: behold, the devil shall cast some of you into prison, that ye may be tried; and ye shall have tribulation ten days: be thou faithful unto death, and I will give thee a crown of life.*

Fear in the Midst of Affliction

Job 3:24-26 - For my sighing cometh before I eat, and my roarings are poured out like the waters. *For the thing which I greatly feared is come upon me, and that which I was afraid of is come unto me.* I was not in safety, neither had I rest, neither was I quiet; yet trouble came.

Job 9:27-28 - If I say, I will forget my complaint, I will leave off my heaviness, and comfort myself: *I am afraid of all my sorrows*, I know that thou wilt not hold me innocent.

Job 23:13-17 - But he is in one mind, and who can turn him? And what his soul desireth, even that he doeth. For he performeth the thing that is appointed for me: and many such things are with him. *Therefore am I troubled at his presence: when I consider, I am afraid of him. For God maketh my heart soft, and the Almighty troubleth me*: because I was not cut off before the darkness, neither hath he covered the darkness from my face.

Psalm 107:23-29 - They that go down to the sea in ships, that do business in great waters; these see the works of the LORD, and his wonders in the deep. For he commandeth, and raiseth the stormy wind, which lifteth up the waves thereof. They mount up to the heaven, they go down again to the depths: *their soul is melted because of trouble. They* *reel to and fro, and stagger like a drunken man, and are at their wits' end.* Then they cry unto the LORD in their trouble, and he bringeth them out of their distresses. He maketh the storm a calm, so that the waves thereof are still.

Psalm 119:39 - *Turn away my reproach which I fear*: for thy judgments are good.

Jonah 1:4-5 - But the LORD sent out a great wind into the sea, and there was a mighty tempest in the sea, so that the ship was like to be broken. *Then the mariners were afraid, and cried every man unto his god*, and cast forth the wares that were in the ship into the sea, to lighten it of them. But Jonah was gone down into the sides of the ship; and he lay, and was fast asleep.

Mark 4:35, 37-40 - And the same day, when the even was come, he saith unto them, Let us pass over unto the other side . . . . And there arose a great storm of wind, and the waves beat into the ship, so that it was now full. And he was in the hinder part of the ship, asleep on a pillow: and they awake him, and say unto him, *Master, carest thou not that we perish?* And he arose, and rebuked the wind, and said unto the sea, Peace, be still. And the wind ceased, and there was a great calm. *And he said unto them, Why are ye so fearful? How is it that ye have no faith?* (See also Matthew 8:23-27; Luke 8:22-25)

Matthew 14:28-31 - And Peter answered him and said, Lord, if it be thou, bid me come unto thee on the water. And he said, Come. And when Peter was come down out of the ship, he walked on the water, to go to Jesus. *But when he saw the wind boisterous, he was afraid; and beginning to sink, he cried, saying, Lord, save me. And immediately Jesus stretched forth his hand, and caught him, and said unto him, O thou of little faith, wherefore didst thou doubt?*

Acts 27:14-20 - *But not long after there arose against it a tempestuous wind*, called Euroclydon. *And when the ship was caught*, and could not bear up into the wind, we let her drive. And running under a certain island which is called Clauda, we had much work to come by the boat: which when they had taken up, they used helps, undergirding the ship; *and, fearing lest they should fall into the quicksands*, strake sail, and so were driven. And we being exceedingly tossed with a tempest, the next day they lightened the ship; and the third day we cast out with our own hands the tackling of the ship. *And when neither sun nor stars in many days appeared, and no small tempest lay on us, all hope that we should be saved was then taken away.*

2 Corinthians 7:5 - For, when we were come into Macedonia, *our flesh had no rest, but we were troubled on every side; without were fightings, within were fears.*

I Will Fear No Evil

Psalm 23:1-6 - *The LORD is my shepherd; I shall not want.* He maketh me to lie down in green pastures: he leadeth me beside the still waters. He restoreth my soul: he leadeth me in the paths of righteousness for his name's sake. *Yea, though I walk through the valley of the shadow of death, I will fear no evil: for thou art with me; thy rod and thy staff they comfort me.* Thou preparest a table before me in the presence of mine enemies: thou anointest my head with oil; my cup runneth over. Surely goodness and mercy shall follow me all the days of my life: and I will dwell in the house of the LORD for ever.

Psalm 3:1-8 - LORD, how are they increased that trouble me! Many are they that rise up against me. Many there be which say of my soul, There is no help for him in God. Selah. *But thou, O LORD, art a shield for me; my glory, and the lifter up of mine head. I cried unto the LORD with my voice, and he heard me out of his holy hill.* Selah. *I laid me down and slept; I awaked; for the LORD sustained me. I will not be afraid of ten thousands of people, that have set themselves against me round about. Arise, O LORD; save me, O my God: for thou hast smitten all mine enemies upon the cheek bone; thou hast broken the teeth of the ungodly. Salvation belongeth unto the LORD: thy blessing is upon thy people.* Selah.

Psalm 27:1-6 - *The LORD is my light and my salvation; whom shall I fear? The LORD is the strength of my life; of whom shall I be afraid?* When the wicked, even mine enemies and my foes, came upon me to eat up my flesh, they stumbled and fell. *Though an host should encamp against me, my heart shall not fear: though war should rise against me, in this will I be confident. One thing have I desired of the LORD, that will I seek after; that I may dwell in the house of the LORD all the days of my life, to behold the beauty of the LORD, and to enquire in his temple. For in the time of trouble he shall hide me in his pavilion: in the secret of his tabernacle shall he hide me; he shall set me up upon a rock.* And now shall mine head be lifted up above mine enemies round about me: *therefore will I offer in his tabernacle sacrifices of joy; I will sing, yea, I will sing praises unto the LORD.*

Psalm 46:1-3 - *God is our refuge and strength, a very present help in trouble. Therefore will not we fear*, though the earth be removed, and though the mountains be carried into the midst of the sea; though the waters thereof roar and be troubled, though the mountains shake with the swelling thereof. Selah.

Psalm 56:1-13 - *Be merciful unto me, O God*: for man would swallow me up; he fighting daily oppresseth me. Mine enemies would daily swallow me up: for they be many that fight against me, O thou most High. *What time I am afraid, I will trust in thee. In God I will praise his word, in God I have put my trust; I will not fear what flesh can do unto me.* Every day they wrest my words: all their thoughts are against me for evil. They gather themselves together, they hide themselves, they mark my steps, when they wait for my soul. S hall they escape by iniquity? *In thine anger cast down the people, O God. Thou tellest* *my wanderings: put thou my tears into thy bottle: are they not in thy book? When I cry unto thee, then shall mine enemies turn back: this I know; for God is for me. In God will I praise his word: in the LORD will I praise his word. In God have I put my trust: I will not be afraid what man can do unto me. Thy vows are upon me, O God: I will render praises unto thee. For thou hast delivered my soul from death: wilt not thou deliver my feet from falling, that I may walk before God in the light of the living?*

Psalm 118:4-6 - Let them now that fear the LORD say, that his mercy endureth for ever. *I called upon the LORD in distress: the LORD answered me, and set me in a large place. The LORD is on my side; I will not fear: what can man do unto me?*

Isaiah 12:1-3 - And in that day thou shalt say, *O LORD, I will praise thee: though thou wast angry with me, thine anger is turned away, and thou comfortedst me. Behold, God is my salvation; I will trust, and not be afraid: for the LORD JEHOVAH is my strength and my song; he also is become my salvation.* Therefore with joy shall ye draw water out of the wells of salvation.

Hebrews 13:5-6 - Let your conversation be without covetousness; and be content with such things as ye have: *for he hath said, I will never leave thee, nor forsake thee. So that we may boldly say, The Lord is my helper, and I will not fear what man shall do unto me.*

Afraid of Man

Proverbs 29:25 - *The fear of man bringeth a snare: but whoso putteth his trust in the LORD shall be safe.*

Psalm 18:1-6 - *I will love thee, O LORD, my strength. The LORD is my rock, and my fortress, and my deliverer; my God, my strength, in whom I will trust; my buckler, and the horn of my salvation, and my high tower. I will call upon the LORD, who is worthy to be praised: so shall I be saved from mine enemies.* The sorrows of death compassed me, *and the floods of ungodly men made me afraid.* The sorrows of hell compassed me about: the snares of death prevented me. *In my distress I called upon the LORD, and cried unto my God: he heard my voice out of his temple, and my cry came before him, even into his ears.*

Psalm 31:13-17 - *For I have heard the slander of many: fear was on every side*: while they took counsel together against me, they devised to take away my life. *But I trusted in thee, O LORD: I said, Thou art my God. My times are in thy hand: deliver me from the hand of mine enemies, and from them that persecute me. Make thy face to shine upon thy servant: save me for thy mercies' sake. Let me not be ashamed, O LORD; for I have called upon thee*: let the wicked be ashamed, and let them be silent in the grave.

Psalm 64:1-4 - *Hear my voice, O God, in my prayer: preserve my life from fear of the enemy.* *Hide me from the secret counsel of the wicked; from the insurrection of the workers of iniquity*: who whet their tongue like a sword, and bend their bows to shoot their arrows, even bitter words: that they may shoot in secret at the perfect: suddenly do they shoot at him, and fear not.

Isaiah 51:12-13 - *I, even I, am he that comforteth you: who art thou, that thou shouldest be afraid of a man that shall die, and of the son of man which shall be made as grass; and forgettest the LORD thy maker, that hath stretched forth the heavens, and laid the foundations of the earth; and hast feared continually every day because of the fury of the oppressor, as if he were ready to destroy?* And where is the fury of the oppressor?

Genesis 26:6-7 - And Isaac dwelt in Gerar: and the men of the place asked him of his wife; *and he said, She is my sister: for he feared to say, She is my wife; lest, said he, the men of the place should kill me for Rebekah*; because she was fair to look upon.

Genesis 32:6-7, 9-12 - And the messengers returned to Jacob, saying, We came to thy brother Esau, and also he cometh to meet thee, and four hundred men with him. *Then Jacob was greatly afraid and distressed*: and he divided the people that was with him, and the flocks, and herds, and the camels, into two bands . . . . *And Jacob said, O God of my father Abraham, and God of my father Isaac, the LORD which saidst unto me, Return unto thy country, and to thy kindred, and I will deal well with thee*: I am not worthy of the least of all the mercies, and of all the truth, which thou hast shewed unto thy servant; for with my staff I passed over this Jordan; and now I am become two bands. *Deliver me, I pray thee, from the hand of my*

brother, from the hand of Esau: for I fear him, lest he will come and smite me, and the mother with the children. And thou saidst, I will surely do thee good, and make thy seed as the sand of the sea, which cannot be numbered for multitude.

Hebrews 11:23-27 - By faith Moses, when he was born, was hid three months of his parents, because they saw he was a proper child; *and they were not afraid of the king's commandment.* By faith Moses, when he was come to years, refused to be called the son of Pharaoh's daughter; *choosing rather to suffer affliction with the people of God, than to enjoy the pleasures of sin for a season; esteeming the reproach of Christ greater riches than the treasures in Egypt*: for he had respect unto the recompence of the reward. *By faith he forsook Egypt, not fearing the wrath of the king: for he endured, as seeing him who is invisible.*

Deuteronomy 20:8 - And the officers shall speak further unto the people, and they shall say, *What man is there that is fearful and fainthearted? Let him go and return unto his house, lest his brethren's heart faint as well as his heart.*

Judges 6:25-27 - And it came to pass the same night, that the LORD said unto him, Take thy father's young bullock, even the second bullock of seven years old, and throw down the altar of Baal that thy father hath, and cut down the grove that is by it: and build an altar unto the LORD thy God upon the top of this rock, in the ordered place, and take the second bullock, and offer a burnt sacrifice with the wood of the grove which thou shalt cut down. Then Gideon took ten men of his servants, and did as the LORD had said unto him: *and so it was, because he feared his father's household, and the men of the city, that he could not do it by day, that he did it by night.*

Judges 7:1-3, 9-15 - Then Jerubbaal, who is Gideon, and all the people that were with him, rose up early, and pitched beside the well of Harod: so that the host of the Midianites were on the north side of them, by the hill of Moreh, in the valley. And the LORD said unto Gideon, The people that are with thee are too many for me to give the Midianites into their hands, lest Israel vaunt themselves against me, saying, Mine own hand hath saved me. *Now therefore go to, proclaim in the ears of the people, saying, Whosoever is fearful and afraid, let him return and depart early from mount Gilead. And there returned of the people twenty and two thousand; and there remained ten thousand* . . . . And it came to pass the same night, that the LORD said unto him, Arise, get thee down unto the host; for I have delivered it into thine hand. *But if thou fear to go down, go thou with Phurah thy servant down to the host: and thou shalt hear what they say; and afterward shall thine hands be strengthened to go down unto the host.* Then went he down with Phurah his servant unto the outside of the armed men that were in the host. And the Midianites and the Amalekites and all the children of the east lay along in the valley like grasshoppers for multitude; and their camels were without number, as the sand by the sea side for multitude. And when Gideon was come, behold, there was a man that told a dream unto his fellow, and said, Behold, I dreamed a dream, and, lo, a cake of barley bread tumbled into the host of Midian, and came unto a tent, and smote it that it fell, and overturned it, that the tent lay along. *And his fellow answered and said, This is nothing else save the sword of Gideon the son of Joash, a man of Israel: for into his hand hath God delivered Midian, and all the host. And it was so, when Gideon heard the telling of the dream, and the interpretation thereof, that he worshipped, and returned into the host of Israel, and said, Arise; for the LORD hath delivered into your hand the host of Midian.*

1 Samuel 3:11-15 - And the LORD said to Samuel, Behold, I will do a thing in Israel, at which both the ears of every one that heareth it shall tingle. In that day I will perform against Eli all things which I have spoken concerning his house: when I begin, I will also make an end. For I have told him that I will judge his house for ever for the iniquity which he knoweth; because his sons made themselves vile, and he restrained them not. And therefore I have sworn unto the house of Eli, that the iniquity of Eli's house shall not be purged with sacrifice nor offering for ever. And Samuel lay until the morning, and opened the doors of the house of the LORD. *And Samuel feared to shew Eli the vision.*

1 Samuel 7:7-8 - And when the Philistines heard that the children of Israel were gathered together to Mizpeh, the lords of the Philistines went up against Israel. *And when the children of Israel heard it, they were afraid of the Philistines. And the children of Israel said to Samuel, Cease not to cry unto the LORD our God for us, that he will save us out of the hand of the Philistines.*

1 Samuel 15:24-26 - And Saul said unto Samuel, I have sinned: *for I have transgressed the commandment of the LORD, and thy words: because I feared the people, and obeyed their voice.* Now therefore, I pray thee, pardon my sin, and turn again with me, that I may worship the LORD. And Samuel said unto Saul, I will not return with thee: for thou hast rejected the word of the LORD, and the LORD hath rejected thee from being king over Israel.

1 Samuel 17:4-11, 24 - And there went out a champion out of the camp of the Philistines, named Goliath, of Gath, whose height was six cubits and a span. And he had an helmet of brass upon his head, and he was armed with a coat of mail; and the weight of the coat was five thousand shekels of brass. And he had greaves of brass upon his legs, and a target of brass between his shoulders. And the staff of his spear was like a weaver's beam; and his spear's head weighed six hundred shekels of iron: and one bearing a shield went before him. And he stood and cried unto the armies of Israel, and said unto them, Why are ye come out to set your battle in array? Am not I a Philistine, and ye servants to Saul? Choose you a man for you, and let him come down to me. If he be able to fight with me, and to kill me, then will we be your servants: but if I prevail against him, and kill him, then shall ye be our servants, and serve us. And the Philistine said, I defy the armies of Israel this day; give me a man, that we may fight together. *When Saul and all Israel heard those words of the Philistine, they were dismayed, and greatly afraid . . . . And all the men of Israel, when they saw the man, fled from him, and were sore afraid.*

1 Samuel 21:10-13 - *And David arose, and fled that day for fear of Saul, and went to Achish the king of Gath.* And the servants of Achish said unto him, Is not this David the king of the land? Did they not sing one to another of him in dances, saying, Saul hath slain his thousands, and David his ten thousands? *And David laid up these words in his heart, and was sore afraid of Achish the king of Gath. And he changed his behaviour before them, and feigned himself mad in their hands, and scrabbled on the doors of the gate, and let his spittle fall down upon his beard.*

1 Samuel 23:1-4 - Then they told David, saying, Behold, the Philistines fight against Keilah, and they rob the threshingfloors. Therefore David enquired of the LORD, saying, Shall I go and smite these Philistines? And the LORD said unto David, Go, and smite the Philistines, and save Keilah.

And David's men said unto him, Behold, we be afraid here in Judah: how much more then if we come to Keilah against the armies of the Philistines? Then David enquired of the LORD yet again. And the LORD answered him and said, Arise, go down to Keilah; for I will deliver the Philistines into thine hand.

Isaiah 57:11 - *And of whom hast thou been afraid or feared, that thou hast lied, and hast not remembered me, nor laid it to thy heart?* Have not I held my peace even of old, and thou fearest me not?

Jeremiah 38:19-20 - *And Zedekiah the king said unto Jeremiah, I am afraid of the Jews that are fallen to the Chaldeans, lest they deliver me into their hand, and they mock me.* But Jeremiah said, They shall not deliver thee. *Obey, I beseech thee, the voice of the LORD*, which I speak unto thee: so it shall be well unto thee, and thy soul shall live.

Nehemiah 6:5-18a, 19 - Then sent Sanballat his servant unto me in like manner the fifth time with an open letter in his hand; wherein was written, It is reported among the heathen, and Gashmu saith it, that thou and the Jews think to rebel: for which cause thou buildest the wall, that thou mayest be their king, according to these words. And thou hast also appointed prophets to preach of thee at Jerusalem, saying, There is a king in Judah: and now shall it be reported to the king according to these words. Come now therefore, and let us take counsel together. Then I sent unto him, saying, There are no such things done as thou sayest, but thou feignest them out of thine own heart. *For they all made us afraid, saying, Their hands shall be weakened from the work, that it be not done. Now therefore, O God, strengthen my hands.* Afterward I came unto the house of Shemaiah the son of Delaiah the son of Mehetabeel, who was shut up; and he said, Let us meet together in the house of God, within the temple, and let us shut the doors of the temple: for they will come to slay thee; yea, in the night will they come to slay thee. *And I said, Should such a man as I flee?* And who is there, that, being as I am, would go into the temple to save his life? I will not go in. *And, lo, I perceived that God had not sent him*; but that he pronounced this prophecy against me: for Tobiah and Sanballat had hired him. *Therefore was he hired, that I should be afraid, and do so, and sin, and that they might have matter for an evil report, that they might reproach me. My God, think thou upon Tobiah and Sanballat according to these their works, and on the prophetess Noadiah, and the rest of the prophets, that would have put me in fear.* So the wall was finished in the twenty and fifth day of the month Elul, in fifty and two days. *And it came to pass, that when all our enemies heard thereof, and all the heathen that were about us saw these things, they were much cast down in their own eyes: for they perceived that this work was wrought of our God.* Moreover in those days the nobles of Judah sent many letters unto Tobiah, and the letters of Tobiah came unto them. For there were many in Judah sworn unto him . . . . Also they reported his good deeds before me, and uttered my words to him. *And Tobiah sent letters to put me in fear.*

Matthew 2:19-23 - But when Herod was dead, behold, an angel of the Lord appeareth in a dream to Joseph in Egypt, saying, Arise, and take the young child and his mother, and go into the land of Israel: for they are dead which sought the young child's life. And he arose, and took the young child and his mother, and came into the land of Israel. *But when he heard that Archelaus did reign in Judaea in the room of his father Herod, he was afraid to go thither: notwithstanding, being warned of God in a dream, he turned* *aside into the parts of Galilee*: and he came and dwelt in a city called Nazareth: that it might be fulfilled which was spoken by the prophets, He shall be called a Nazarene.

John 7:13 - *Howbeit no man spake openly of him* [of the Lord Jesus Christ] *for fear of the Jews.*

John 9:20-23 - His parents answered them and said, We know that this is our son, and that he was born blind: but by what means he now seeth, we know not; or who hath opened his eyes, we know not: he is of age; ask him: he shall speak for himself. *These words spake his parents, because they feared the Jews: for the Jews had agreed already, that if any man did confess that he was Christ, he should be put out of the synagogue.* Therefore said his parents, He is of age; ask him.

John 19:38 - And after this Joseph of Arimathaea, *being a disciple of Jesus, but secretly for fear of the Jews*, besought Pilate that he might take away the body of Jesus: and Pilate gave him leave. He came therefore, and took the body of Jesus.

John 20:19 - Then the same day at evening, being the first day of the week, *when the doors were shut where the disciples were assembled for fear of the Jews*, came Jesus and stood in the midst, and saith unto them, Peace be unto you.

Galatians 2:11-13 - But when Peter was come to Antioch, I withstood him to the face, *because he was to be blamed.* For before that certain came from James, he did eat with the Gentiles: *but when they were come, he withdrew and separated himself, fearing them which were of the circumcision. And the other Jews dissembled likewise with him; insomuch that Barnabas also was carried away with their dissimulation.*

Delivered from Fear

Psalm 78:50-53 - He made a way to his anger; he spared not their soul from death, but gave their life over to the pestilence; and smote all the firstborn in Egypt; the chief of their strength in the tabernacles of Ham: *but made his own people to go forth like sheep, and guided them in the wilderness like a flock. And he led them on safely, so that they feared not*: but the sea overwhelmed their enemies.

Leviticus 26:3-4, 6 - *If ye walk in my statutes, and keep my commandments, and do them*; then I will give you rain in due season, and the land shall yield her increase, and the trees of the field shall yield their fruit . . . . *And I will give peace in the land, and ye shall lie down, and none shall make you afraid*: and I will rid evil beasts out of the land, neither shall the sword go through your land.

Psalm 34:1-6 - *I will bless the LORD at all times: his praise shall continually be in my mouth. My soul shall make her boast in the LORD*: the humble shall hear thereof, and be glad. *O magnify the LORD with me, and let us exalt his name together. I sought the LORD, and he heard me, and delivered me from all my fears.* They looked unto him, and were lightened: and their faces were not ashamed. *This poor man cried, and the LORD heard him, and saved him out of all his troubles.*

Psalm 91:1-10 - *He that dwelleth in the secret place of the most High shall abide under the shadow of the Almighty. I will say of the LORD, He is my refuge and my fortress: my God; in him will I trust. Surely he shall deliver thee from the snare of the fowler, and from the noisome pestilence. He shall cover thee with his feathers, and under his wings shalt thou trust: his truth shall be thy shield and buckler. Thou shalt not be afraid for the terror by night; nor for the arrow that flieth by day; nor for the pestilence that walketh in darkness; nor for the destruction that wasteth at noonday. A thousand shall fall at thy side, and ten thousand at thy right hand; but it shall not come nigh thee. Only with thine eyes shalt thou behold and see the reward of the wicked. Because thou hast made the LORD, which is my refuge, even the most High, thy habitation; there shall no evil befall thee, neither shall any plague come nigh thy dwelling.*

Psalm 112:6-8 - Surely he shall not be moved for ever: the righteous shall be in everlasting remembrance. *He shall not be afraid of evil tidings: his heart is fixed, trusting in the LORD. His heart is established, he shall not be afraid*, until he see his desire upon his enemies.

Proverbs 1:20-23, 33 - Wisdom crieth without; she uttereth her voice in the streets: she crieth in the chief place of concourse, in the openings of the gates: in the city she uttereth her words, saying, How long, ye simple ones, will ye love simplicity? And the scorners delight in their scorning, and fools hate knowledge? Turn you at my reproof: behold, I will pour out my spirit unto you, I will make known my words unto you . . . . *But whoso hearkeneth unto me shall dwell safely, and shall be quiet from fear of evil.*

Proverbs 3:13-26 - *Happy is the man that findeth wisdom, and the man that getteth understanding.* For the merchandise of it is better than the merchandise of silver, and the gain thereof than fine gold. She is more precious than rubies: and all the things thou canst desire are not to be compared unto her. Length of days is in her right hand; and in her left hand riches and honour. Her ways are ways of pleasantness, and all her paths are peace. She is a tree of life to them that lay hold upon her: *and happy is every one that retaineth her.* The LORD by wisdom hath founded the earth; by understanding hath he established the heavens. By his knowledge the depths are broken up, and the clouds drop down the dew. My son, let not them depart from thine eyes: keep sound wisdom and discretion: so shall they be life unto thy soul, and grace to thy neck. *Then shalt thou walk in thy way safely, and thy foot shall not stumble. When thou liest down, thou shalt not be afraid: yea, thou shalt lie down, and thy sleep shall be sweet. Be not afraid of sudden fear, neither of the desolation of the wicked, when it cometh. For the LORD shall be thy confidence, and shall keep thy foot from being taken.*

Isaiah 14:1-4 - *For the LORD will have mercy on Jacob, and will yet choose Israel, and set them in their own land*: and the strangers shall be joined with them, and they shall cleave to the house of Jacob. And the people shall take them, and bring them to their place: and the house of Israel shall possess them in the land of the LORD for servants and handmaids: and they shall take them captives, whose captives they were; and they shall rule over their oppressors. *And it shall come to pass in the day that the LORD shall give thee rest from thy sorrow, and from thy fear, and from the hard bondage wherein thou wast made to serve*, that thou shalt take up this proverb against the king of Babylon, and say, How hath the oppressor ceased! The golden city ceased!

Isaiah 54:11-17 - *O thou afflicted, tossed with tempest, and not comforted, behold, I will lay thy stones with fair colours, and lay thy foundations with sapphires.* And I *will make thy windows of agates, and thy gates of carboncles, and all thy borders of pleasant stones.* And all thy *children shall be taught of the LORD; and great shall be the peace of thy children.* In righteousness shalt thou be *established: thou shalt be far from oppression; for thou shalt not fear: and from terror; for it shall not come near thee.* Behold, they shall surely gather together, but not by me: *whosoever shall gather together against thee shall fall for thy sake.* Behold, I have created the smith that bloweth the coals in the fire, and that bringeth forth an instrument for his work; and I have created the waster to destroy. *No weapon that is formed against thee shall prosper; and every tongue that shall rise against thee in judgment thou shalt condemn.* This is the heritage of the *servants of the LORD, and their righteousness is of me, saith the LORD.*

Jeremiah 20:7-13 - O LORD, thou hast deceived me, and I was deceived: thou art stronger than I, and hast prevailed: *I am in derision daily, every one mocketh me.* For since I spake, I cried out, I cried violence and spoil; *because the word of the LORD was made a reproach unto me, and a derision, daily.* Then I said, I will not make mention of him, nor speak any more in his name. But his word was in mine heart as a burning fire shut up in my bones, and I was weary with forbearing, and I could not stay. *For I heard the defaming of many, fear on every side.* Report, say they, and we will report it. All my familiars watched for my halting, saying, Peradventure he will be enticed, and we shall prevail against him, and we shall take our revenge on him. *But the LORD is with me as a mighty terrible one: therefore my persecutors shall stumble, and they shall not* *prevail: they shall be greatly ashamed; for they shall not prosper: their everlasting confusion shall never be forgotten.* But, O LORD *of hosts, that triest the righteous, and seest the reins and the heart, let me see thy vengeance on them: for unto thee have I opened my cause. Sing unto the* LORD, *praise ye the* LORD: *for he hath delivered the soul of the poor from the hand of evildoers.*

Jeremiah 23:3-6 - And I will gather the remnant of my flock out of all countries whither I have driven them, and will bring them again to their folds; and they shall be fruitful and increase. And I will set up shepherds over them which shall feed them: *and they shall fear no more, nor be dismayed, neither shall they be lacking, saith the* LORD. Behold, the days come, saith the LORD, that I will raise unto David a righteous Branch, and a King shall reign and prosper, and shall execute judgment and justice in the earth. *In his days Judah shall be saved, and Israel shall dwell safely: and this is his name whereby he shall be called, THE LORD OUR RIGHTEOUSNESS.*

Jeremiah 30:5-9 - *For thus saith the* LORD; *We have heard a voice of trembling, of fear, and not of peace.* Ask ye now, and see whether a man doth travail with child? *Wherefore do I see every man with his hands on his loins, as a woman in travail, and all faces are turned into paleness?* Alas! For that day is great, so that none is like it: it is even the time of Jacob's trouble; *but he shall be saved out of it. For it shall come to pass in that day, saith the* LORD *of hosts, that I will break his yoke from off thy neck, and will burst thy bonds, and strangers shall no more serve themselves of him: but they shall serve the* LORD *their God, and David their king, whom I will raise up unto them.*

Jeremiah 39:16-18 - Go and speak to Ebedmelech the Ethiopian, saying, Thus saith the LORD of hosts, the God of Israel; Behold, I will bring my words upon this city for evil, and not for good; and they shall be accomplished in that day before thee. *But I will deliver thee in that day, saith the LORD: and thou shalt not be given into the hand of the men of whom thou art afraid. For I will surely deliver thee, and thou shalt not fall by the sword, but thy life shall be for a prey unto thee: because thou hast put thy trust in me, saith the LORD.*

Ezekiel 34:22-29 - *Therefore will I save my flock, and they shall no more be a prey*; and I will judge between cattle and cattle. *And I will set up one shepherd over them, and he shall feed them, even my servant David; he shall feed them, and he shall be their shepherd.* And I the LORD will be their God, and my servant David a prince among them; I the LORD have spoken it. *And I will make with them a covenant of peace, and will cause the evil beasts to cease out of the land: and they shall dwell safely in the wilderness, and sleep in the woods.* And I will make them and the places round about my hill a blessing; and I will cause the shower to come down in his season; there shall be showers of blessing. And the tree of the field shall yield her fruit, and the earth shall yield her increase, *and they shall be safe in their land, and shall know that I am the LORD, when I have broken the bands of their yoke, and delivered them out of the hand of those that served themselves of them. And they shall no more be a prey to the heathen, neither shall the beast of the land devour them; but they shall dwell safely, and none shall make them afraid.* And I will raise up for them a plant of renown, and they shall be no more consumed with hunger in the land, neither bear the shame of the heathen any more.

Ezekiel 39:25-26 - Therefore thus saith the Lord GOD; *Now will I bring again the captivity of Jacob, and have mercy upon the whole house of Israel,* and will be jealous for my holy name; after that they have borne their shame, and all their trespasses whereby they have trespassed against me, *when they dwelt safely in their land, and none made them afraid.*

Micah 4:1-4 - But in the last days it shall come to pass, that the mountain of the house of the LORD shall be established in the top of the mountains, and it shall be exalted above the hills; and people shall flow unto it. And many nations shall come, and say, Come, and let us go up to the mountain of the LORD, and to the house of the God of Jacob; and he will teach us of his ways, and we will walk in his paths: for the law shall go forth of Zion, and the word of the LORD from Jerusalem. And he shall judge among many people, and rebuke strong nations afar off; *and they shall beat their swords into plowshares, and their spears into pruninghooks: nation shall not lift up a sword against nation, neither shall they learn war any more. But they shall sit every man under his vine and under his fig tree; and none shall make them afraid*: for the mouth of the LORD of hosts hath spoken it.

Zephaniah 3:12-14 - I will also leave in the midst of thee an afflicted and poor people, *and they shall trust in the name of the LORD.* The remnant of Israel shall not do iniquity, nor speak lies; neither shall a deceitful tongue be found in their mouth: *for they shall feed and lie down, and none shall make them afraid. Sing, O daughter of Zion; shout, O Israel; be glad and rejoice with all the heart, O daughter of Jerusalem. The LORD hath taken away thy judgments, he hath cast out thine enemy: the king of Israel, even the LORD, is in the midst of thee: thou shalt not see evil any more.*

Luke 1:67-75 - And his father Zacharias was filled with the Holy Ghost, and prophesied, saying, *Blessed be the Lord God of Israel; for he hath visited and redeemed his people, and hath raised up an horn of salvation for us in the house of his servant David*; as he spake by the mouth of his holy prophets, which have been since the world began: *that we should be saved from our enemies, and from the hand of all that hate us; to perform the mercy promised to our fathers, and to remember his holy covenant*; the oath which he sware to our father Abraham, *that he would grant unto us, that we being delivered out of the hand of our enemies might serve him without fear, in holiness and righteousness before him, all the days of our life.*

Romans 8:15-17 - *For ye have not received the spirit of bondage again to fear; but ye have received the Spirit of adoption, whereby we cry, Abba, Father. The Spirit itself beareth witness with our spirit, that we are the children of God*: and if children, then heirs; heirs of God, and joint-heirs with Christ; if so be that we suffer with him, that we may be also glorified together.

Philippians 1:12-14 - But I would ye should understand, brethren, *that the things which happened unto me have fallen out rather unto the furtherance of the gospel*; so that my bonds in Christ are manifest in all the palace, and in all other places; *and many of the brethren in the Lord, waxing confident by my bonds, are much more bold to speak the word without fear.*

2 Timothy 1:7-8 - *For God hath not given us the spirit of fear; but of power, and of love, and of a sound mind. Be not thou therefore ashamed of the testimony of our Lord, nor of me his prisoner: but be thou partaker of the afflictions of the gospel according to the power of God.*

Hebrews 2:14-15 - Forasmuch then as the children are partakers of flesh and blood, he also himself likewise took part of the same; *that through death he might destroy him that had the power of death, that is, the devil; and deliver them who through fear of death were all their lifetime subject to bondage.*

1 John 4:17-19 - Herein is our love made perfect, *that we may have boldness in the day of judgment*: because as he is, so are we in this world. *There is no fear in love; but perfect love casteth out fear: because fear hath torment. He that feareth is not made perfect in love. We love him, because he first loved us.*

Fear as a Judgment from the Lord

Deuteronomy 28:58-60, 63-64a, 65-67 - *If thou wilt not observe to do all the words of this law that are written in this book, that thou mayest fear this glorious and fearful name, THE LORD THY GOD*; then the LORD will make thy plagues wonderful, and the plagues of thy seed, even great plagues, and of long continuance, and sore sicknesses, and of long continuance. *Moreover he will bring upon thee all the diseases of Egypt, which thou wast afraid of; and they shall cleave unto thee* . . . . And it shall come to pass, that as the LORD rejoiced over you to do you good, and to multiply you; so the LORD will rejoice over you to destroy you, and to bring you to nought; and ye shall be plucked from off the land whither thou goest to possess it. And the LORD shall scatter thee among all people . . . . *And among these nations shalt thou find no ease, neither shall the sole of thy foot have rest: but the LORD shall give thee there a trembling heart, and failing of eyes, and sorrow of mind: and thy life shall hang in doubt before thee; and thou shalt fear day and night, and shalt have none assurance of thy life: in the morning thou shalt say, Would God it were even! And at even thou shalt say, Would God it were morning! For the fear of thine heart wherewith thou shalt fear, and for the sight of thine eyes which thou shalt see.*

1 Samuel 28:4-8, 11-12, 15-20 - And the Philistines gathered themselves together, and came and pitched in Shunem: and Saul gathered all Israel together, and they pitched in Gilboa. *And when Saul saw the host of the Philistines, he was afraid, and his heart greatly trembled. And when Saul enquired of the LORD, the LORD answered him not, neither by dreams, nor by Urim, nor by prophets.* Then said Saul unto his servants, Seek me a woman that hath a familiar spirit, that I may go to her, and enquire of her. And his servants said to him, Behold, there is a woman that hath a familiar spirit at Endor. And Saul disguised himself, and put on other raiment, and he went, and two men with him, and they came to the woman by night: and he said, I pray thee, divine unto me by the familiar spirit, and bring me him up, whom I shall name unto thee . . . . Then said the woman, Whom shall I bring up unto thee? And he said, Bring me up Samuel. And when the woman saw Samuel, she cried with a loud voice: and the woman spake to Saul, saying, Why hast thou deceived me? For thou art Saul . . . . And Samuel said to Saul, Why hast thou disquieted me, to bring me up? *And Saul answered, I am sore distressed; for the Philistines make war against me, and God is departed from me, and answereth me no more, neither by prophets, nor by dreams: therefore I have called thee, that thou mayest make known unto me what I shall do. Then said Samuel, Wherefore then dost thou ask of me, seeing the LORD is departed from thee, and is become thine enemy?* And the LORD hath done to him, as he spake by me: for the LORD hath rent the kingdom out of thine hand, and given it to thy neighbour, even to David: *because thou obeyedst not the voice of the LORD,* nor executedst his fierce wrath upon Amalek, therefore hath the LORD done this thing unto thee this day. *Moreover the LORD will also deliver Israel with thee into the hand of the Philistines: and to morrow shalt thou and thy sons be with me: the*

LORD *also shall deliver the host of Israel into the hand of the Philistines. Then Saul fell straightway all along on the earth, and was sore afraid, because of the words of Samuel: and there was no strength in him*; for he had eaten no bread all the day, nor all the night.

Psalm 53:1-6 - *The fool hath said in his heart, There is no God. Corrupt are they, and have done abominable iniquity: there is none that doeth good.* God looked down from heaven upon the children of men, to see if there were any that did understand, that did seek God. *Every one of them is gone back: they are altogether become filthy; there is none that doeth good, no, not one.* Have the workers of iniquity no knowledge? *Who eat up my people as they eat bread: they have not called upon God. There were they in great fear, where no fear was: for God hath scattered the bones of him that encampeth against thee: thou hast put them to shame, because God hath despised them.* Oh that the salvation of Israel were come out of Zion! When God bringeth back the captivity of his people, Jacob shall rejoice, and Israel shall be glad.

Isaiah 24:17-21 - *Fear, and the pit, and the snare, are upon thee, O inhabitant of the earth.* And it shall come to pass, that he who fleeth from the noise of the fear shall fall into the pit; and he that cometh up out of the midst of the pit shall be taken in the snare: for the windows from on high are open, and the foundations of the earth do shake. The earth is utterly broken down, the earth is clean dissolved, the earth is moved exceedingly. The earth shall reel to and fro like a drunkard, and shall be removed like a cottage; and the transgression thereof shall be heavy upon it; and it shall fall, and not rise again. *And it shall come to pass in that day, that the LORD shall punish the host of the high ones that are on high, and the kings of the earth upon the earth.*

Isaiah 33:14 - *The sinners in Zion are afraid; fearfulness hath surprised the hypocrites.* Who among us shall dwell with the devouring fire? Who among us shall dwell with everlasting burnings?

Isaiah 66:3-4 - He that killeth an ox is as if he slew a man; he that sacrificeth a lamb, as if he cut off a dog's neck; he that offereth an oblation, as if he offered swine's blood; he that burneth incense, as if he blessed an idol. *Yea, they have chosen their own ways, and their soul delighteth in their abominations. I also will choose their delusions, and will bring their fears upon them; because when I called, none did answer; when I spake, they did not hear: but they did evil before mine eyes, and chose that in which I delighted not.*

Jeremiah 6:19, 21-26 - Hear, O earth: *behold, I will bring evil upon this people,* even the fruit of their thoughts, *because they have not hearkened unto my words, nor to my law, but rejected it* . . . . *Therefore thus saith the LORD, Behold, I will lay stumblingblocks before this people, and the fathers and the sons together shall fall upon them; the neighbour and his friend shall perish.* Thus saith the LORD, Behold, a people cometh from the north country, and a great nation shall be raised from the sides of the earth. They shall lay hold on bow and spear; they are cruel, and have no mercy; their voice roareth like the sea; and they ride upon horses, set in array as men for war against thee, O daughter of Zion. *We have heard the fame thereof: our hands wax feeble: anguish hath taken hold of us, and pain, as of a woman in travail. Go not forth into the field, nor walk by the way; for the sword of the enemy and fear is on every side. O daughter of my people, gird thee with sackcloth, and wallow thyself in ashes: make thee mourning, as for an only son, most bitter lamentation: for the spoiler shall suddenly come upon us.*

Jeremiah 22:21, 25 - I spake unto thee in thy prosperity; *but thou saidst, I will not hear. This hath been thy manner from thy youth, that thou obeyedst not my voice . . . . And I will give thee into the hand of them that seek thy life, and into the hand of them whose face thou fearest,* even into the hand of Nebuchadrezzar king of Babylon, and into the hand of the Chaldeans.

Jeremiah 42:13-18 - *But if ye say, We will not dwell in this land, neither obey the voice of the LORD your God,* saying, No; but we will go into the land of Egypt, where we shall see no war, nor hear the sound of the trumpet, nor have hunger of bread; and there will we dwell: and now therefore hear the word of the LORD, ye remnant of Judah; Thus saith the LORD of hosts, the God of Israel; *If ye wholly set your faces to enter into Egypt, and go to sojourn there; then it shall come to pass, that the sword, which ye feared, shall overtake you there in the land of Egypt, and the famine, whereof ye were afraid, shall follow close after you there in Egypt; and there ye shall die. So shall it be with all the men that set their faces to go into Egypt to sojourn there; they shall die by the sword, by the famine, and by the pestilence: and none of them shall remain or escape from the evil that I will bring upon them. For thus saith the LORD of hosts, the God of Israel; As mine anger and my fury hath been poured forth upon the inhabitants of Jerusalem; so shall my fury be poured forth upon you, when ye shall enter into Egypt: and ye shall be an execration, and an astonishment, and a curse, and a reproach; and ye shall see this place no more.*

Jeremiah 48:42-44 - *And Moab shall be destroyed from being a people, because he hath magnified himself against the LORD. Fear, and the pit, and the snare, shall* *be upon thee, O inhabitant of Moab, saith the LORD. He that fleeth from the fear shall fall into the pit; and he that getteth up out of the pit shall be taken in the snare: for I will bring upon it, even upon Moab, the year of their visitation, saith the LORD.*

Jeremiah 49:2, 4-5, 23-24, 28-29 - *Therefore, behold, the days come, saith the LORD, that I will cause an alarm of war to be heard in Rabbah of the Ammonites*; and it shall be a desolate heap, and her daughters shall be burned with fire: then shall Israel be heir unto them that were his heirs, saith the LORD . . . . Wherefore gloriest thou in the valleys, thy flowing valley, O backsliding daughter? *That trusted in her treasures, saying, Who shall come unto me? Behold, I will bring a fear upon thee, saith the Lord GOD of hosts, from all those that be about thee; and ye shall be driven out every man right forth; and none shall gather up him that wandereth* . . . . Concerning Damascus. *Hamath is confounded, and Arpad: for they have heard evil tidings: they are fainthearted; there is sorrow on the sea; it cannot be quiet. Damascus is waxed feeble, and turneth herself to flee, and fear hath seized on her: anguish and sorrows have taken her, as a woman in travail .* . . . Concerning Kedar, and concerning the kingdoms of Hazor, which Nebuchadrezzar king of Babylon shall smite, thus saith the LORD; Arise ye, go up to Kedar, and spoil the men of the east. Their tents and their flocks shall they take away: they shall take to themselves their curtains, and all their vessels, and their camels; *and they shall cry unto them, Fear is on every side.*

Jeremiah 50:9, 11, 13-14, 16 - *For, lo, I will raise and cause to come up against Babylon an assembly of great nations from the north country*: and they shall set themselves in array against her; from thence she shall be taken:

their arrows shall be as of a mighty expert man; none shall return in vain . . . . *Because ye were glad, because ye rejoiced, O ye destroyers of mine heritage, because ye are grown fat as the heifer at grass, and bellow as bull* . . . . *Because of the wrath of the LORD it shall not be inhabited, but it shall be wholly desolate*: every one that goeth by Babylon shall be astonished, and hiss at all her plagues. Put yourselves in array against Babylon round about: all ye that bend the bow, shoot at her, spare no arrows: *for she hath sinned against the LORD* . . . . Cut off the sower from Babylon, and him that handleth the sickle in the time of harvest: *for fear of the oppressing sword they shall turn every one to his people, and they shall flee every one to his own land.*

Jeremiah 51:29-32 - *And the land shall tremble and sorrow: for every purpose of the LORD shall be performed against Babylon, to make the land of Babylon a desolation without an inhabitant. The mighty men of Babylon have forborn to fight, they have remained in their holds: their might hath failed; they became as women*: they have burned her dwellingplaces; her bars are broken. One post shall run to meet another, and one messenger to meet another, to shew the king of Babylon that his city is taken at one end, and that the passages are stopped, and the reeds they have burned with fire, *and the men of war are affrighted.*

Lamentations 3:42-47 - *We have transgressed and have rebelled: thou hast not pardoned. Thou hast covered with anger, and persecuted us: thou hast slain, thou hast not pitied. Thou hast covered thyself with a cloud, that our prayer should not pass through. Thou hast made us as the offscouring and refuse in the midst of the people. All our enemies have opened their mouths against us. Fear and a snare is come upon us, desolation and destruction.*

Ezekiel 11:8-10 - *Ye have feared the sword; and I will bring a sword upon you, saith the Lord GOD. And I will bring you out of the midst thereof, and deliver you into the hands of strangers, and will execute judgments among you. Ye shall fall by the sword; I will judge you in the border of Israel*; and ye shall know that I am the LORD.

Ezekiel 30:8-9, 13, 19 - And they shall know that I am the LORD, *when I have set a fire in Egypt, and when all her helpers shall be destroyed. In that day shall messengers go forth from me in ships to make the careless Ethiopians afraid, and great pain shall come upon them, as in the day of Egypt: for, lo, it cometh* . . . . Thus saith the Lord GOD; I will also destroy the idols, and I will cause their images to cease out of Noph; and there shall be no more a prince of the land of Egypt: *and I will put a fear in the land of Egypt* . . . . *Thus will I execute judgments in Egypt*: and they shall know that I am the LORD.

Ezekiel 32:9-10 - *I will also vex the hearts of many people, when I shall bring thy destruction among the nations, into the countries which thou hast not known. Yea, I will make many people amazed at thee, and their kings shall be horribly afraid for thee, when I shall brandish my sword before them; and they shall tremble at every moment, every man for his own life, in the day of thy fall.*

Luke 21:25-26 - *And there shall be signs in the sun, and in the moon, and in the stars; and upon the earth distress of nations, with perplexity; the sea and the waves roaring; men's hearts failing them for fear, and for looking after those things which are coming on the earth: for the powers of heaven shall be shaken.*

Proverbs 10:24 - *The fear of the wicked, it shall come upon him*: but the desire of the righteous shall be granted.

Other booklets in

The God's Own Word Series

GOD'S OWN WORD
On The Fear of the Lord

Chapter Contents

The Fear of the Lord
The Terror of the Lord –
Because of His Glory
The Fear of God's People –
Because His Hand Is with Them
Learning to Fear the Lord
The Benefits of Fearing the Lord
If You Will Not Fear the Lord
The Terror of the Lord –
Because of Our Sin

GOD'S OWN WORD
To Those Who Are Mistreated

Chapter Contents

Do Good to Those Who Mistreat You
Love Your Enemies
Maintain a Tender Heart and
a Forgiving Spirit
Rejoice When You Suffer
for Christ's Sake
Wait with Patience upon the Lord's
Deliverance
Trust the Lord to Repay Those
Who Mistreat You

www.shepherdingtheflock.com

Other books from
Shepherding the Flock Ministries

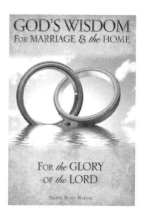

GOD'S WISDOM For MARRIAGE & the HOME

A comprehensive study of what the Word of God teaches about marriage and the home, including chapters on:
The Priority of Marriage
The Permanency of Marriage
The Purpose of Marriage
Cleaving unto Thy Wife (Parts 1 & 2)
An Help Meet for Him (Parts 1 & 2)
Love One Another
One-Flesh Unity
(446 pages)

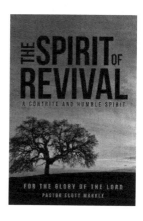

THE SPIRIT OF REVIVAL
A CONTRITE AND HUMBLE SPIRIT

A Biblical study of the inseparable relationship between Biblical humility and spiritual revival, including studies in Isaiah 57:15-21; James 4:1-10; 2 Chronicles 7:12-14; Psalm 51:1-19; and Isaiah 66:1-5. *(200 pages)*

www.shepherdingtheflock.com

4883931R00048

Made in the USA
San Bernardino, CA
12 October 2013